OUR LATE NIGHT

and

A THOUGHT
IN THREE PARTS

Other works by Wallace Shawn

screenplays:

My Dinner with André
by Wallace Shawn and André Gregory

Marie and Bruce
by Wallace Shawn and Tom Cairns

translations:

The Mandrake by Niccolò Machiavelli

The Master Builder by Henrik Ibsen

The Threepenny Opera by Bertolt Brecht

opera libretti:

In the Dark, music by Allen Shawn

The Music Teacher, music by Allen Shawn

plays:

The Hotel Play

Marie and Bruce

Aunt Dan and Lemon

The Fever

The Designated Mourner

Grasses of a Thousand Colors

OUR LATE NIGHT

and

A THOUGHT
IN THREE PARTS

Wallace Shawn

THEATRE COMMUNICATIONS GROUP
NEW YORK
2008

Our Late Night and *A Thought in Three Parts* is published by
Theatre Communications Group, Inc., 520 Eighth Avenue, 24th Floor,
New York, NY 10018-4156

Our Late Night was published previously by the Royal Court Theatre, London, in
1999 and by William Targ Editions, New York, in 1984; *A Thought in Three Parts* was
published previously in *Wallace Shawn: Four Plays* by Farrar, Straus and Giroux, New
York, in 1991 and by PAJ Publications in *Wordplays 2: New American Drama*,
Baltimore, in 1982.

This publication is made possible in part with public funds from the New York State
Council on the Arts, a State Agency.

TCG books are exclusively distributed to the book trade by Consortium Book
Sales and Distribution.

LIBRARY OF CONGRESS CATALOGING-IN-PUBLICATION DATA
Shawn, Wallace.
Our late night ; and, A thought in three parts : two plays / Wallace Shawn.—1st ed.
p. cm.
ISBN 978-1-55936-322-8
I. Shawn, Wallace. Thought in three parts. II. Title. III. Title: Thought in three parts.
PS3569.H387O9 2008
812.54—dc22   2007034916

Book design and composition by Lisa Govan
Cover design by Mark Melnick
Cover photo © ballyscanlon/Photonica/GettyImages
Author photo © Bill Pierce/Time & Life Pictures/GettyImages

First Edition, May 2008

EARLY TEACHERS

Our Late Night 1972 – 1975

André Gregory
Gerry Bamman
Tom Costello
John Ferraro
Saskia Noordhoek Hegt
Karen Ludwig
Angela Pietropinto
Larry Pine
Kathleen Tolan

Contents

INTRODUCTION

By the Author

ix

OUR LATE NIGHT

I

A THOUGHT IN THREE PARTS

3 I

AFTERWORD

By the Author

79

INTRODUCTION

IT'S EASIER TO SLEEP if your head is elevated, and so people use pillows. If you want to attach one piece of cloth to another piece of cloth, a sewing machine can be extremely helpful, and that's why Isaac M. Singer made sewing machines. But why do people make and use what we call "artistic" objects?

It's a question that seems particularly puzzling if you make such objects yourself, in a way devoting your life to it, without quite knowing why you're doing it.

George Gershwin might possibly have wondered to himself, "Why do I write songs?" and yet, as soon as he wrote them, many, many of his fellow humans were eager to sing them, and others were dying to listen to them, and when they heard them, they all felt better and happier, so even though, in a way, those facts don't quite answer the original question, they don't quite explain Gershwin's drive to write music, still, in another way, what more of an answer could Gershwin possibly have wanted?

Everyone knows that if you're hungry and depressed, a little ice cream can bring a moment of relief, and that's why we like it.

Our Late Night was completed in 1972, *A Thought in Three Parts* in 1976. I think I presented them to the world with many of the same feelings that Gershwin had when he presented his songs—in each case I had given my all and done my best to make something that I found pleasing. To me, they were more than pleasing.

Although I'd already written a few other plays, *Our Late Night* was the first to be publicly performed. It was done in New York City in 1975 by André Gregory's group, the Manhattan Project. The production of the play was absolutely brilliant. But the level of hostility that boiled up from the small audience was seriously disturbing. It was almost sickening. *A Thought in Three Parts* was done in New York the following year. It was performed for three weeks for the subscribers of a large theater, but it was not officially "opened" or presented to the critics. This time the audience was not so much hostile as stricken, miserable—they seemed hurt and baffled. (Footnote: the official United States opening of *A Thought in Three Parts* finally happened in 2007, in Austin, Texas, by Rubber Rep.)

Every day I wake up wondering what happened to these plays. They haven't caught on, apparently, even after all this time. And the years I spent writing them—what were those years? Were they like the years that recovered alcoholics describe—"lost years" spent wandering in a drunken haze from one night's incomprehensible encounter with someone or other to the next night's horrible barroom brawl?

Not long ago, I made a film with a group of people, and we'd poured a significant portion of our lives into making it, along with quite a bit of thought and passion, and finally it was shown at a film festival. And when the screening of the film was over, a moderator asked the audience if anyone had any questions for the filmmakers. Almost instantly, a man spoke up from the center of the auditorium. "Yes, I have a question," he said in a loud voice, "*What was the point of that?*" Now, let's note that his question could have meant two different things. He might have been wondering what the point was for us in making the film. Or he might have been asking what point there could possibly have been for him in watching it. But in a way, I feel that my whole life seems to revolve around the fact that I'm crawling through the streets every day unable to answer either version of that question about anything I do.

You have to understand, I do read these plays myself every few years. I read them, I change a few words, I improve a few lines, and I note one more time that I'm obviously different from a lot of other people, because they haven't liked these plays, and I do, even though I don't *seem* that different from all the other people who are out there—I like the same foods that other people like, I admire the same actors that they admire, I listen to the same songs on the radio and sing them to myself as I walk down the street.

People always say that "tastes differ," and that that's just a fact. A lot of people like spinach. Many fewer like dandelion greens. When certain people take their clothes off in public, they're worshipped and rewarded, while others are arrested or taken to an insane asylum. But if you have a stake in the answer, it's hard not to ask, "Why the spinach? Why not the greens?"

Surprisingly—and for me, in a way, it makes my life even harder to understand—there are a group of people now who like what I do, and at this very moment a wonderful publisher has decided to publish this book, and here it is. Should I say something about the book to you, dear reader?

I do remember that when I was a boy it seemed terribly enjoyable to put a little bit of everything that was there in my mother's kitchen into a bowl, and then I would mix it up with a big spoon—but in the end it actually didn't taste very good, not even to me. Without quite realizing that that was what I was doing, I think I've learned to do some equivalent of that mixing-bowl trick in the theater, and I've even learned how to come up with some mixtures which I myself find delicious, though admittedly they don't have universal appeal the way my mother's creamed chicken once did, for example.

To begin with, my plays are a response to the world we live in—I mean, I only say that because it might well seem that they take place on Mars. And like other people who write for the theater, I'm writing about how people interact in the world—you know, society, power, even sometimes classes of society, in a way—but also about people's inner states. *A Thought in Three Parts* really is a meditation: three approaches to something are being contrasted, held up to the audience for their inspection. The degree of "naturalism" of the plays is hard to define—I think maybe the guests in *Our Late Night* may not be quite real, for example. Maybe they simply express what's going on inside the hosts as they enter into an awful, terrifying downward spiral. It's clearly central to the story that they live very high up in a gigantic building that overlooks a giant city.

A play is a wonderful pile-up of bodies, lights, sets, gestures, clothes, nudity, music, dance, and running through it all and driving it all is a stream of words, sentences. Words and sentences are aesthetic materials, and a purpose which I think one would have to call aesthetic is the governing element in the book you're holding. I'm playing with sentences the way a child plays with matches—because they're unpredictable. Sentences make up a sort of jungle in which I seem to be living. Anyway, I'm stirring up and mixing up various elements in order to create an artistic object, an object that exists for the purpose of being contemplated. The object doesn't mean one particular thing, it doesn't say one particular thing—it's just sort of there, and you can walk around it, look at it from different angles, enjoy it in whatever way you like, and take from it what you like.

The contemplation of an artistic object can induce a sort of daytime dream, one might say, and perhaps it's somewhat odd for a play to have that intention, at least in comparison to a painting, for example. Agnes Martin's paintings put the viewer into a trance, while Bertolt Brecht's plays were specifically designed to wake people up. Let's just say that I'm trying to square the circle by doing both things at once.

I wonder if the daytime dreams induced by artistic objects may not be really rather necessary for people, as nighttime dreams unquestionably are. If they weren't necessary, then why would every culture on earth invent music, songs, poetry, what have you? Perhaps it's the case that, in order to live, we must process our experience first rationally, and then irrationally. But if such dreams are actually necessary in fact, that goes some way to explaining the nasty atmosphere that hovered in those rooms when my plays were being performed. In other words, at night we can all create for ourselves the dreams that we need, but the creation of the artistic objects that stimulate our daytime dreams is contracted out to a particular group of people—and in our society it's a self-appointed group. So naturally the various dreams that we dream at night are not criticized by anybody—there are no reviews in the Land of Nod—nor do we need to defend our dreams or make any claims for them. But as we all find ourselves in the frustrating situation that most of the artistic objects we need and depend on for our daytime dreams must be made by other people, it's not surprising that we're finicky, critical and, sometimes, even angry when these objects are presented to us—we're constantly complaining, like diners in a restaurant who repeatedly send bad-tasting dishes back to the kitchen. And then, perhaps inevitably, centuries ago, analysts of art brought the concepts of "good" and "bad" into the conversation, and most of us, as irritable diners, frequently use this vocabulary in discussing our artistic meals, although it often merely adds to the prevailing confusion, because a parsnip is not really a "bad" carrot, it's a different vegetable.

So. What type of dreams do *you* enjoy? There are clearly different categories of dreams that vie for primacy in each human soul. Some are dreams of conquest, victory, revenge, supremacy, power. Others are dreams of sensuality, beauty, joy, kindness and love. Artistic objects are not brainwashing machines. They have influence, not power. But I think we're influenced by our daytime dreams, just as much as we're influenced by our family and friends and our personal experiences. So to me it's reasonable to think that a world in which Chuang Tzu and George Eliot are widely read will be less dangerous than a world in which people only read sadistic stories or military magazines.

Certain theorists definitely disagree with that opinion. In fact, there are people who dwell obsessively on the fact that an exposure to "art" did *not* prevent certain famous men from doing horrible things. I feel I've been frequently reminded, for example, that the Nazi leader Reinhard Heydrich played Mozart on the violin during the same period in which he planned the extermination of the Jews of Europe. But my speculation on this, if I may offer one, is that perhaps, because of his history and who he was, Commander Heydrich did not fully absorb the human possibilities that others have grasped through listening to the music of Mozart. Similarly, the young English major Seung-Hui Cho killed thirty-two people in a famous massacre at a college in Virginia, even though a kindly professor of English had given him private tutorials in creative writing and had even tried to ask him about his own problems. She did her best, but Cho was too deeply trapped in the quicksand of his own mind, and the lessons in creative writing didn't save him. He didn't hear enough, or understand enough, of what his teacher was trying to tell him. Mozart, being a composer of music rather than a supernatural creature from outer space, was not up to the task of convincing Reinhard Heydrich to get off the path he was on and move to another one. But just as the failure of Cho's teacher can hardly lead us to say that no kindly teacher has ever helped or saved a student, so it seems preposterous to leap from Mozart's inability to reconstruct Reinhard Heydrich to the claim that composers, painters and writers have not influenced the world by offering humanity their wisdom and their vision of what life could be.

Dreams can help, although they don't make their points in a direct way, and sometimes no one can say for sure exactly what their points really are. Dreams can even agitate for change, or for a better world, sometimes simply by offering people a glimpse of something agreeable that might be pursued—or crystallizing into a nightmare something awful that ought to be avoided. Dreams are actually involved in a serious battle. Despite a certain lightness in their presentation, they're not joking.

February 2008

OUR LATE NIGHT

Our Late Night was first performed in New York by the Manhattan Project at Joseph Papp's New York Shakespeare Festival/The Public Theater on January 9, 1975. It was produced by Lyn Austin. It was directed by André Gregory, designed by Douglas Schmidt, with costumes by Ara Gallant. The cast was:

ANNETTE	Angela Pietropinto
LEWIS	Larry Pine
GRANT	Gerry Bamman
KRISTIN	Karen Ludwig
JIM	John Ferraro
TONY	Tom Costello
SAMANTHA	Saskia Noordhoek Hegt

The play was first produced in London by the Royal Court Theatre (in residence at the New Ambassadors Theatre), in a "production without decor" on October 21, 1999. It was directed by Caryl Churchill, with creative assistance by Antony McDonald, Mauricio Elginaya, Johanna Town and Paul Arditti. The cast was:

ANNETTE	Nancy Crane
LEWIS	Ewan Stewart
GRANT	Andrew Woodall
KRISTIN	Ingrid Lacey
JIM	Jonathan Cullen
TONY	Stephen Dillane
SAMANTHA	Jacqueline Defferary

Evening. An apartment—high, very high, above a giant city. Yellowish light, from a lamp. A sense that the room might tip over; things might fall—or slip. Lewis and Annette are dressed for a party, kissing. They are in their thirties. An atmosphere that is almost ceremonial—calm, solemn.

ANNETTE *(Removing hairs from Lewis's jacket)*: . . . hairs all over
   you . . .
LEWIS: Let me see your face. *(He stares at her face)*
ANNETTE: The people will be here . . .
LEWIS *(He stares)*: I'm going to kiss you again.
ANNETTE: Wait—slowly. *(He kisses her)*

   (The lights dim. Annette moves to a window. Lights up, as before.)

LEWIS: Do you think I should be a woman tonight?
ANNETTE: Is that what you want, Lewis?
LEWIS: Yes—I think so. Daylight doesn't become me as a
   woman, but it's night now. I'll be a woman.

(He brushes his hair.)

(As a woman) May I?

ANNETTE: Go ahead.

(He goes to her slowly, touches her face from behind, caresses it.)

Go ahead.

(He kisses her. Then they stand silently looking out the window.)

LEWIS *(No longer as a woman)*: You really love me, don't you.
ANNETTE: Stop asking me that, Lewis.
LEWIS: You can't get enough of me. Each moment of my presence is a privilege for you. *(Pause)* What are you looking at?
ANNETTE: The back of the city.

(Lights out. They speak in darkness.)

The buildings—
LEWIS: Yes—
ANNETTE: —standing below us like stiff children, with swollen knees and crabbed-up knuckles—can't move—

(In the darkness, while Annette speaks, Lewis and Annette's guests silently take their places. Kristin is the youngest, Grant is the oldest. Grant takes a place by Annette. Kristin is with Lewis, near the window. Tony is with Jim. Samantha sits alone. With no pause, still in darkness, Annette addresses Grant:)

I like those pants.

(Lights up, bright and white. The middle of a party.)

(Not pausing before she speaks) I've never seen any like them.

GRANT: Well I made them myself! Ha ha—did you know I could sew?

(Simultaneous conversations begin between Grant and Annette, Kristin and Lewis, and Tony and Jim.)

ANNETTE *(To Grant)*: Such a stinging, strong color. Do they stick to your legs?

GRANT: They cling on tight. I love the way they feel—I cut them twenty times to get them just the way I wanted.

KRISTIN *(To Lewis)*: We said good-bye to the masters, and first we ran. In our jackets, and carrying our books. And then we found the place, for meeting, to stop, to eat. We had a radio. But what was it called? Oh yeah—

JIM *(To Tony)*: I keep trying to get my windows repaired, but it's so expensive to buy boards these days. You know, even plain slats! They're taxed by the yard! Goddamn it, it really gets to me!

TONY: Yeah, it *is* infuriating.

(Now we hear only one conversation at a time. Other conversations may continue, but, if they do, they can't be heard.)

KRISTIN: It was called Sandwich Lane.

LEWIS: Oh.

KRISTIN: Sandwich Lane. *(Pause)* And they all came. *(Pause)* Sally, Billy, Tissue, Cunt, Pole, and Face.

LEWIS: Oh—yes—

KRISTIN: Our mouths drooped, we ate—we danced—

LEWIS: Yes—

KRISTIN: It was hot—the sun—the grass—Sally took off her shirt!

LEWIS: Oh no!

KRISTIN: Then Face did—then I did! The boys were ill— they were gasping for breath!

LEWIS: My God!

KRISTIN: Then Sally went wild, she started unzipping, she took everything off—pants—underwear—we were throwing it around! My zipper was stuck! I was scared to show my hairs!

LEWIS: Oh my God—

KRISTIN: Then we chased the boys and grabbed them, and stripped them. We even felt them—they felt like fish!

LEWIS: Oh God—

KRISTIN: Then Pole put his fingers in each of the girls—he wanted to give us a thrill!

LEWIS: Oh no—

KRISTIN: And we tried some kissing, and rolling around— and then we lay in the grass and farted. I think we threw some food—and spilled the orange juice.

LEWIS: You did?

KRISTIN: And Face brought Billy off by hand—oh God—it seemed so strange!

LEWIS: Aha ha ha—

(They both laugh for a long time.)

Aha ha ha ha ha. Ah yes—yes—that's really amusing— yes indeed—aha ha ha—a fine story! Oh yes . . . *(A long pause)* Aha ha ha. Do you like our view?

KRISTIN: Yeah—fantastic. It's so high, it almost makes me want to throw up!

LEWIS: Yes—yes—that's right—I know what you mean!

TONY *(To Jim)*: Because after all, you know, I feel that certain trends in society are becoming—well—almost disturbing—
JIM: Really? You do?
TONY: Well, dishonesty, for example—and lying . . .
JIM: Lying? Oh yes, that's very disturbing.
TONY: Because you see, yesterday a man told me that he'd eaten steak and fried potatoes at a famous fish and clam house. Now, that wasn't true.
JIM: Oh that's right, and that kind of thing happens just all the time, just every day . . .
TONY: So why do they do it? Why do they?
JIM: Well—I really don't know! I wish I knew, Goddamn it!
TONY *(Introducing Jim and Samantha)*: But do you know my friend Samantha?

(Tony moves to look out a window, then goes into the bathroom, starting to feel a bit ill.)

LEWIS *(To Kristin)*: Yeah—but now how about that elevator ride up here! Huh? Now isn't that something?
KRISTIN: Oh God! It's so fast! And that little screaming sound!
LEWIS: Do you know—when you get to the top—you feel so pinched!—so tight—your head feels so thin and dizzy!
KRISTIN: Oh God!
LEWIS: You know, I sometimes almost—aha!—feel drained—eheh!—or I almost feel that I'm going to have—an orgasm! No! Really! I do! Aha ha ha—
KRISTIN: Oh God—oh God—you're such a character! Aha ha ha! Ha ha ha!
LEWIS: Ahahaha! Ahahahaha! Jesus, you know, I'd really—like to lick—your tits—ahaha—

9

KRISTIN: No—really? Would you really like to do that?

LEWIS: I'd like to put my hand up your dress, just to feel the sweat. I want—I want to see—inside your mouth.

KRISTIN: Yes?

LEWIS: I'd like—I'd like to stuff myself inside you, stuff myself in till you coughed.

KRISTIN: I don't know. Do you think you'd be satisfied?

LEWIS: They say there's a release at the end . . .

KRISTIN: Yes, but sometimes it doesn't work out, and then you're just left feeling drippy and sad. See, that's how you feel already. *(Pause)*

LEWIS: So—I can't persuade you?

KRISTIN: No. Be serious. Do you think I want to spoil my face and my hair? Do you think I want to do "hands and feet" with a rotten banana? Do you think I want to do "rounders" with little darts and whistles? These are my nipples. They're very sensitive. Do you follow me?

LEWIS: Yes. Oh yes. Yes, I see how you feel . . .

JIM *(To Samantha)*: Aha ha ha—but you don't seem too interested. I hope I'm not too boring for you, really I do. Ha ha ha—telling you about myself—aha ha ha—but I'll tell you one more thing about myself, and, you know, this may seem so foolish and absurd to you, but still— do you know what I like to do—now I'm speaking frankly—more than anything in the world? Aha ha— I'll bet you can't guess. *(She doesn't respond)* Well, you see, I live alone, and well, you won't believe this, but frankly, what I like to do more than anything in the world is to put on an apron, rush about in my little kitchen, and prepare a great big meal for myself! *(She still doesn't respond)* Now you know, when I started, I just didn't know the first thing about cooking. Ha ha—I used to put the salt in the sugar, the sugar in the

salt—aha ha ha ha—oh Lord—Lord—but by now—
well, it's amazing—but I'm really beginning to get the
hang of it. I mean it! I can whip up a cake or a soufflé
in no time flat! And—do you know what?—I've even
managed to work out a few new recipes of my own!
Really, maybe you should come over some time and try
some of my special things. What do you think? Ha ha
ha. And do you know what my favorite dish of all is? I'll
bet you can't guess. Yes—it's cooked rice, with beans!
(A long pause) No! Really! It is! Aha ha ha . . . ha ha . . .

SAMANTHA *(After a long pause)*: Listen to me. I want to stop
you now, because all of what you've said is of no impor-
tance to me. I'm sorry. You see, the things you've been
talking about . . . Look—you see, I've drunk wine that
was made from sperm. Now, that's all I need to know
about it. And I've lived off pigeon stew, made from raw
pigeons, cooked with their brains. You see, there's no
point in talking anymore about these things.

JIM: Ha ha. No—of course not! I was just talking so aim-
lessly—it was absurd! Ha ha— *(Pause)* Did you come
to the party with that fellow who introduced us? With
Tony? He seems like a very nice person!

(Pause.)

SAMANTHA: Listen to me. Do you want to talk with me
tonight?

JIM: Of course.

SAMANTHA: Then listen carefully to me. You see, you don't
have to know about these things. If you don't want to
know them, then you can tell me.

JIM: Yes—of course . . .

(A long pause. Then she speaks.)

SAMANTHA: I see beyond my eyes.

JIM *(Quietly)*: Oh—really?

SAMANTHA: I live inside my face, see. Beyond my face.

JIM *(Quietly)*: Oh . . . you do? . . .

SAMANTHA: I know babies I'm not supposed to know, gifts that are hidden as surprises, places behind the sofa where I don't belong.

JIM: Oh—

SAMANTHA: I've read letters from women who couldn't any longer breathe or give milk. I've felt their lips while they were drying up—lips sometimes smeared with blood— *(A long pause)* Boys pulled my hair and kicked me. They came into me from behind. They left me bleeding. Then they left me by the ocean. I swam alone under the moon, and looked at my breasts in the water. Then I lay on the sand on my back and watched the waves, and the gulls, and the crabs. *(Pause)* And in the light before the dawn, the living bands of the birds— the orange birds, the yellow birds, the blue birds, the green birds—took me in, and fed me. I lived in their nests, naked and happy, stretched out, or curled up, in the worms and straw.

(A long pause.)

JIM: Really—remarkable—eheh heh . . . But you look so pale. Are you sure you're well? I mean—I hope you're not ill!

(Pause.)

SAMANTHA: Ill? Yes . . . Well—you see—earlier in the evening—I was in there—that's the bathroom . . .

JIM: Yes—I noticed that.

SAMANTHA: I coughed up my dinner, into the sink. It looked like there were some white feathers in it too, and a piece of a wing.

JIM: Oh—

SAMANTHA: And some little bones, too. I tried to pick them out. *(Pause)* Can you smell that I threw up?

JIM: No—not at all.

SAMANTHA: Good. Have you been in their bathroom too tonight?

JIM: No.

SAMANTHA: It's nicely decorated. *(Pause)* How do you like this dress? It's a strange shade of green, isn't it?

JIM: Yes—it suits you.

SAMANTHA: Thank you. You know, I'd like to take a bath in their tub—maybe with my clothes on. A warm bath, I mean. Would you like to watch me?

JIM: Yes—I'd like to watch you. But if you wore your clothes, you might catch cold.

SAMANTHA: Would you like to watch me without my clothes?

JIM: Well—I'm not really sure. I might become aroused.

SAMANTHA: Mmm—don't hurt anyone's feelings.

JIM: All right.

SAMANTHA: I'm going to keep dry. I'll put on my coat . . . I'm sorry, I can't concentrate anymore.

JIM: No—no—that's fine—eheh heh heh . . .

(Tony emerges from the bathroom and approaches Jim as Samantha drifts away from him. Annette and Grant continue to talk.)

GRANT: Well—have you tasted my "red breast of dog" fondue?

ANNETTE: We had cheese the last time.

GRANT: I cook the meat in the sauce. That way it's fresher.

(Pause.)

ANNETTE: Your hands are so white.

GRANT: Except for the warts. They've always been that way. My mother talked about it.

ANNETTE: Long fingers. I'll bet they know how to probe, to open.

GRANT: They slip in, like big mackerels.

ANNETTE: Do they thrash about, and crack the walls?

GRANT: No—they just slowly wave their tails.

TONY *(To Jim, speaking about Samantha)*: Yes—an original girl—ha ha! Yes—I met her through a friend of Cox, you know.

JIM: Oh really? I know Cox!

TONY: Yes—I assumed you did. I used to work for Cox, actually.

JIM: What? You did?

TONY: Yes, I did. I did. I certainly did. Ha ha ha. But tell me—you knew him—did you like him?

JIM: Well, he seemed like a fine man.

TONY: Did he? That's interesting. Ha ha ha. You see, I found him rather a swine.

JIM: Oh—really?

TONY: Yes—I always felt he'd treated me rather shabbily, if you know what I mean.

JIM: Is that so! . . . Yes . . .

TONY: He didn't appreciate me, you see.

JIM: Really—

TONY: But you liked him a great deal, didn't you? I can tell. That's fascinating.

JIM: Yes—yes—I always rather admired him, really. Yes. I did.

TONY: Yes that's fascinating, isn't it? Fascinating. Fascinating. Many people do admire him, tremendously. He has a very great deal of charm, of course. And his wife's a cute piece of ass. I ought to know—I've laid her more than once.

JIM: Really?

TONY: Yes—she took quite an interest in me when I was working for her husband. We used to meet in a little room over a café—The Living Mink, it was called . . . Ha ha ha . . . She was really crazy about me till I started making little jokes about her tummy. Ha ha ha! It was a cute little tummy, really. But I used to pretend it was a little drum and play little tunes on it. Ha ha ha! Aha ha ha ha ha!

JIM: Ha ha ha! Yes! That's very funny!—Good Lord! Little tunes! Aha ha ha ha—

GRANT *(To Annette)*: Because I eat anything. I don't care what—I ate artichokes and olives before I was two. They tasted good to me.

ANNETTE: And human flesh?

GRANT: What about human flesh?

ANNETTE: Have you ever thought about what it would be like to eat the flesh off a human finger—or off the palm of a hand?

GRANT: What are you saying?

JIM *(To Tony)*: So I said, "Why play games? If you take off your panties, I'll take off my briefs. I mean, tennis is tennis, we've had our fun, and now it's time to pull down the net and see who can fly."

ANNETTE: I like you a lot. I could take you up to a room on the roof. There are a few sofas up there, and a small kitchen . . .

GRANT: No. I can't.

TONY (*Chuckling lightly, to Jim*): Aha ha ha—the tropics. The tropics. Let me tell you—that's a funny part of the world down there—let me tell you—or at any rate, it certainly had a strange effect on me—brother!—aha ha—

JIM: Oh—really? What kind of strange effect?

TONY: Well, there was a sort of strange incident that occurred to me, actually—

JIM: Oh—really? There was? What happened?

TONY: Well, it's not that interesting; but it was odd . . .

JIM: No, tell me about it. I'd really like to hear about it.

TONY: Really?

JIM: Yes.

TONY: Well, as I say, it's not that interesting. But it was odd. It really was odd. (*Pause*) You see, I was there in the tropics—and it was on business of course—way out in the tropics—and I had to go out into the most remote areas and introduce myself to the people who lived there . . . Well, one day I knocked on the door of this isolated little hut—and there was really no other habitation for miles around—and inside the hut in this sweltering heat—it was just overpowering—there was an enormous woman lying on a bed—well, it wasn't a bed, it was really just a filthy mattress lying on the floor—probably filled with worms—

JIM: My goodness—

TONY: —and the woman was just lying there, behind a rotting old refrigerator, and there was just one yellow old sheet covering her, and underneath that—underneath that she was completely naked—the most enormous woman I'd ever seen in my life! And she was sweating so profusely, you could hardly believe it. Well, I took off my jacket and began to give my little speech— explaining about my work, what I was doing out there—and all of a sudden she took off her glasses, and she was begging me to lay her, in a way that was unmistakable—she had to have me. Well—I stood there and thought for a moment—but I just had to do it—it seemed too unique to resist! So I took off my pants, and got in underneath that sheet and put in my tool. Well, she was terribly slippery, she began to rock back and forth, and she—she moved so violently that my tool fell out three times! And then when she finally came, she let out these great elephant moans that shook the hut! And she was kissing me warmly and gently all over my face—her mouth was so big I felt almost enclosed—but I kissed her back, and when our mouths met, it was as if I was merging with a beautiful ocean. It was like waves were quietly lapping, everything was calm. For a long while we kissed and kissed, and I forgot about time. But there were some bristles on her face that kept scratching me, and suddenly I became somehow upset, or frightened, I began to panic—

JIM: Good Lord! . . .

TONY: —I had to get away! I pretended I was just going out to get the two of us some fruit from out of her garden, but as soon as I got out there I got into my little jeep, and I drove away as fast as I could. A few minutes later I'd reached my hotel. I ran through the lobby, up the stairs, and into my suite. My wife was in the bathroom taking a shower. I broke in on her. Her breasts were glistening in the water—the nipples were so firm, so tiny, so bright. I immediately got stiff—I had to have her! I rammed my rod into her, sore as it was. She was taken aback—we'd never made love in the shower before, and it was almost impossible—my wife and I are completely different heights!—so we went into the bedroom and climbed on the bed, soaking it with water. Our four-year-old daughter was running around the suite, playing with some friends. We could hear them shouting and laughing as we finished it off. But as soon as we stopped, I felt that sensation in my prick—in a second I was hard—I still wanted more! I savaged into my wife again, just as she was sitting up and putting on her clothes. I almost hurt her lips with my teeth, my mouth was open so wide. My prick was in agony—but my wife loved it—she loved it—loved it! She was like a pool of honey, with delicate, scented cries rising to the surface. Her lips were so hot, they almost burned my cheeks. She began to cry out, with these powerful, piercing, pig-like squeals. The children heard them, so they knocked on our door. I quickly came, then jumped out of the bed, threw on a bathrobe, went to the door, smiled at the children, then closed the door again. My prick was so hot, I went into the bathroom and tried to pour cold water on it, while my wife fingered herself and went on moaning on the bed. Then I put on a bathing suit and ran out of the suite and out of the hotel. My rod was hard again. There was a huge forest near the hotel, and I ran into it. There were pine needles under my feet—my chest and face were getting scratched. All of a sudden I started to cry out, to scream. I screamed and screamed as I ran. And then I came to a lake, and I took out my prick and started to whack it. I whacked and whacked, but I couldn't come. I scratched at my chest and legs with my nails, but it didn't help. Then I threw myself onto the ground, and I lay in the ooze and slime at the edge of the lake—still wearing my trunks—and I rubbed myself into the sand till I finally came, a few tiny drops of bloody pain.

My cries were coming less frequently now. And then night started falling. The sky grew cold. I was covered with gooseflesh, and black with dirt. A few birds landed right in front of me, I was lying so still. I wanted to touch them, to kiss them. In my prick, I could feel that sensation coming back—I knew that I wanted to come again, but that the pain would be too intense. I didn't know what to do. Slowly I crawled back to the hotel. My wife was waiting nervously. I asked her to suck me, gently, but she was horrified at the sight of my cock, and the filth all over me. I took a bath. I couldn't eat—not a bite—not a thing. I lay on the bed, and my wife sucked me, for an hour, gently, but I didn't get hard till finally for a moment at the end, when I brought out my final drop. After that, I covered my face with my pillow and let out some stifled sobs; I felt dizzy, as if I was hurtling through a misshapen darkness, but I knew that when I landed, it would start again, that sensation in my prick, and never stop, never leave me alone—I tried to fall asleep, but every time I was about to drift off, the realization that it would all begin again soon brought me up with a jolt. My wife tried to comfort me, but I couldn't bear to be touched or even approached, and I barked at her unpleasantly until she went away. And then I just held on to my pillow, covering my ears, and finally, after hours—and I really thought those hours would never end—I cried myself to sleep, still hugging that pillow for dear life, and I was still hugging it, close to my ears, when I woke up the next morning.

(A long pause.)

JIM: My God—er—and to think that I'd planned to go to the tropics—on my vacation!

TONY: Excuse me. *(He approaches Samantha)*

19

(Simultaneous conversations now break out between Grant and Jim, Tony and Samantha, and Kristin and Lewis. The conversations of Grant and Jim and Tony and Samantha more or less cover the earlier part of Lewis's speech.)

GRANT *(To Jim)*: Ha ha—that was really quite a story he was telling—very very interesting.

JIM: Yes—yes it certainly was. *(Pause)* Ha ha—of course— ha ha—to you, we're all just transparent, aren't we? Ha ha—I mean—you see right through us!

GRANT: No—on the contrary—no, on the contrary, the more I learn, the less confident I feel.

JIM: Is that right? . . .

TONY *(To Samantha)*: Well—are you all right?—er—how are you doing?—ha ha—

SAMANTHA: How can you ask me that?

TONY: Well, why shouldn't I ask you?—ha ha—

SAMANTHA: I'm not feeling better.

TONY: Oh—gosh—that's too bad. Is it still your stomach?

SAMANTHA: I'm restless. I want something else. Why don't you calm me down, for God's sake? I need something from you.

TONY: All right. All right. Let me get at you, Sam. It's all right. *(He touches her)*

LEWIS *(To Kristin)*: You see, it never stopped snowing there, so that the people just stayed in their stone houses all day and never came out. They lived mostly on these white corn pellets which had been beaten into a mash and then frozen, and which would then be melted in with some fresh snow and a kind of preserved, thick butter, which they thawed out in these black metal pots. They also drank water—it had a kind of metallic taste—and sometimes they used some dried fruits. *(Pause)* Occasionally they would go out to the lake of ice, late in the afternoon, if a seal had been spotted. The women would come too, and the children, and everyone would go out and sit silently by the black and greenish water, in that strange half-light which seems to carry within itself its own almost uncanny hazy blur or absence of focus—and they would all watch while the two head men would struggle through the unfrozen hole, and then, when they had found the seal, and pulled it out, the two men would wrestle to see which one would win the animal for himself. And then one of them would win, and then he would take the seal by its tail and swing its head against a block of ice. They only found five or six seals a year, and it wasn't the meat that was most important. It was the teeth, which they divided, following a complicated sort of a system, and then the teeth were used in exchange, as a supplementary form of wealth. A can of teeth was stolen mysteriously once, and the people broke into feverish rashes— a woman was said to have laughed out loud for a week, and hate-filled feuds began which can never die down.

(Pause.)

KRISTIN *(From far away)*: Please. Don't you see? My face is turning white with liquid heat. And those leeches on his body are red and white kisses. *(Waking up, looking at Jim)*

(Grant and Jim have approached Kristin and Lewis.)

GRANT: Well, how are you doing, Lewis? *(To Kristin and Jim)* Oh—ha ha—do you two know each other?

JIM: Of course, we've met before! But we've hardly had a chance to talk tonight.

LEWIS: Ha ha. Yes—well—how are you, Grant? How's your work been going these days?

GRANT: Well—not badly, not badly. I do my best. *(Looking out the window)* Yes—it's just marvelous—don't you think so? I never get over this view, and that's the truth.

JIM *(To Kristin)*: Ha ha—Well!—how have you been?

KRISTIN: Oh—been! Been! Ha ha ha! Yeah—I've been pretty well. Fine. Fine. Pretty well. Pretty well.

TONY *(Fingering Samantha)*: Can't I help you any more, Sam? I want to help you. I want to. I really want to. *(Pause)* Is this enjoyable for you?

SAMANTHA: No.

TONY: Is this enjoyable?

SAMANTHA: No.

TONY: Is this more enjoyable?

SAMANTHA: No. No. Get those filthy bandages out of me.

(Pause. She feels ill.)

TONY: Sam—are you all right? Did I hurt you?

SAMANTHA: Of course not, Tony. Little weepy man. Little chocolate man. Little hamburger Tony. You only got yourself lost and wet in those great big hairy old doors down there. *(Pause)* Do you want to put your tongue in my mouth, and let me suck it?

TONY: No.

SAMANTHA: Then I want to go home. It's late, and I'm not feeling better. Will you take me back to my apartment?

(Pause.)

TONY: Good God—do you think you're sick? *(He suddenly feels very ill)* But I'm sicker than you. *(Pause)* My throat and my stomach are burning. No—I can't move, Sam. I think I'll throw up. I've got to sit. Here. No. Don't touch me.

(Tony sits. Samantha remains where she is. As Jim and Kristin talk, Grant approaches Tony and Samantha.)

JIM: Well—are you going to come down to my house tonight?
KRISTIN: Well—do you think I should?
JIM: Yes—I think so.
KRISTIN: Why should I come?
JIM: It's down by the beach. We could walk right out my door and go for a swim. Now doesn't that sound nice?
KRISTIN: Yes, but wouldn't it be cold?
JIM: Then we could run inside.
KRISTIN: But—do you think we'd be naked?
JIM: Well—we might be.
KRISTIN: But the bed would be sandy . . .
JIM: It's not sandy. It's sort of nice and warm, and sort of sweet.
KRISTIN: Do you jerk off into it sometimes, onto the sheets?
JIM: No—I only jerk off onto the beach.
KRISTIN: Yes, but look—I don't even know what kinds of things you like—you know? *(Pause)* I like to use jelly on my face—the kind that burns.
JIM: Oh—I don't know about that.
KRISTIN: It's wet, but the burns go deep. They go into death.
JIM: Death?
KRISTIN: You have to keep it on. But I wipe it when it starts to ache. It gets red.
JIM: The burns must do harm.
KRISTIN: You have to keep your face from pinching off. The strips go down your face, but you shouldn't touch them . . .

JIM: It burns till you wipe it?

KRISTIN: If we keep on fucking, I won't wipe it.

JIM: I have some sores on my face and lips, so I don't think—

KRISTIN: Not your face then. Maybe your ass. Or behind your knees.

JIM: But what is the—

KRISTIN: Because of the taste. You'll get the taste even if I put a bit on your legs. See, just wait. You just start fucking, and you keep going, up and down, and then the taste gets hard. It goes right in your mouth, and you know how hard it is. You can't even close your mouth then. You know how metal feels. You can't really move after that, but you just keep fucking. And then it's *not* hard, and it starts to pour out over you, it just pours out, like hot lava. Don't worry. I'll put a little bit inside your dick. I know what I'm doing. I won't hurt you.

JIM: It seems frightening. Why go so far with this?

KRISTIN: I'm a person. Get it? I do things. Do you want them? This is my cunt. Do you want it?

JIM: Yes—yes—but do you need these techniques? Are they really—necessary?

KRISTIN: What kind of enjoyment do you want, Jim?

(Tony is feeling increasingly ill.)

GRANT: Well, it was fine. Yes. The masturbation was satisfactory—of course I didn't feel all the penises myself. We used warps with handles for the women, and then needles and water, for vomiting.

TONY: Were the children brave, in general?

GRANT: Well, some of the younger ones felt some pain when we extracted their fluids, and there was a bit of bleeding—not much, not much . . .

TONY: Did you use the base of the legs?

GRANT: Oh, I didn't want to do that.

LEWIS (*Interjecting from a distance, simultaneously with Grant*): Boys don't use their legs.

TONY: What?

LEWIS: I said I don't think that boys use their legs at all.

GRANT (*Simultaneously with Lewis*): Well, at an early stage— well, at an early stage, actually, neither boys nor girls use their legs. But then, later on, boys and girls use their legs more or less equally. But we were dealing directly with the genitals at that point, of course.

TONY: Yes, but then what happened to their eyes, in the end?

GRANT: Well, their eyes were almost always brighter, actually.

TONY: And their mouths?

GRANT: Their mouths?—well—ha ha—they usually got quite a soaking! Ha! Aha ha!

TONY: And you closed the anus?

GRANT: Well—eheh—we did our best.

TONY: But why? I don't understand.

GRANT: Well again, to prevent the release of moisture.

TONY: And isn't nutrition quite an important factor? I've heard that nutrition is important, too.

GRANT: Of course. Of course. It's crucial, you see. But we don't really know—we don't really know enough about the specific effects of different elements—not yet, you see. My God, it's frightening. And there are some awful stories. Well, one of them happened to me, in fact. Ugh—I hate to think about it. It was because of eating eggs. Ugh. You see, we'd been working all day, and for dinner my wife made a tiny casserole of spinach and hard-boiled eggs—well, the eggs were the mistake, you see—spinach doesn't matter . . . Well, we were in the middle of dinner, and we were chatting along about something or other, and all of a sudden I saw something pink start to fall from her nostrils. And just at the same moment, she started to move sort of restlessly in her chair, because she began to feel something running down her stockings. When she suddenly stood up, it was pouring out of her. Ugh. It took an hour to stop it.

TONY: My God—

GRANT: It was messy, my dear. Messy messy. You know what I mean.

KRISTIN: Do you know about gagging?

JIM: No! No! Look, I just want to hold you, to touch you. Please! Help me!

KRISTIN: You fucking asshole!

(She gives a cry and falls into tears. She prepares to leave. Jim falls silent. Kristin puts on her coat. She doesn't leave, but continues to weep.)

TONY: No, but tell me, Doctor—you know that sometimes—sometimes I—I like to stroke my own daughter. You know those golden hairs that children have on their legs? They excite me.

GRANT: Ha ha—yes! Well—ha ha—I have a daughter, too, so I know what you mean. Those hairs excite everyone! My God, you know, I have a recurring dream about my daughter.

TONY: Really?

GRANT: Yes. Yes. It begins with a dream of myself asleep. God—it's so unbelievably vivid. I'm lying in bed, and she comes and puts her fingers, with those cold pearl nails, through my hair, and around my ear, and around my neck. And then she touches me with her lips, under my eye, kissing me and kissing me, repeatedly. And then I always wake up, and the covers are soaked, and

my gooey thigh is growing cold from what we used to
call—the witch's kiss . . .

(A long pause.)

TONY: Excuse me.

*(Tony goes to the bathroom and begins to vomit, as Kristin
continues weeping.)*

GRANT *(To Samantha)*: My own feminine side is cold and girl-
ish, and whenever I'm a girl, I'm always a blond. A sort
of hot-summer-day-sticky, honey-sugar-syrup blond.
I tie blue ribbons in my hair, and play with hoops and
rings, and do hopscotch and upside-down games on the
bars, and chanting jump rope. And then I like to wet all
the ends of my hair, and rub them, so they'll be slippy
and springy, and then I run in the grass like bouncy sun-
shine.

SAMANTHA: Don't touch me.

(A long silence, with sounds of weeping and vomiting.)

GRANT: You know, there was a time when night itself seemed
to be so magical . . . *(Laughs silently. Pause)* They told us
we needed to be "saved." *(A slight laugh)* I remember
one day—one spring day—spring had opened up all
the doors and windows. The bugs flew in with the
sunny breezes—they ignored the screens— *(Laughs)*
We thought we knew what it meant to be happy. I sat
on my cot and played with my mother's ring, a tiny
flower with petals of gold and silver and red and black
and white. I didn't need to get out, or leave my room.
Because I knew that night would be coming soon, and

stopping at my station, and shutting up my house. And all day long, the green leaves and the rancid lawns sent their smells through the light, and waited to be snuffed. And then it was night, and I cried when my mother came with a good-night kiss; she brought me a dish of ice cream on a tray. *(A slight laugh. A long pause)* Are you content? Are you accepting me?

SAMANTHA: No. No.

GRANT: Touch me.

SAMANTHA: No. I can't. I don't want to.

(She touches him. He kisses her.)

GRANT: I think I can help you. I think I can help you.

(Tony comes out of the bathroom.)

TONY *(To Annette)*: Where's my coat? I'm sorry—I cleaned up the mess in there.

ANNETTE: That's all right—really. *(Lights out)* It's all right.

(Immediately, lights up, from the window. A different light. Time has passed. It's very late at night. The guests are gone. Lewis and Annette are not quite asleep—but they're not quite awake either.)

LEWIS: Why don't you try to sleep?

ANNETTE: I'm listening—

LEWIS: Yes—

ANNETTE: To the street, see, there's cars down there, and big cans of stuff—they're kicking them—oo—lots of boys on bicycles—

LEWIS *(Staring at Annette)*: Who put you together? How come you're alive? How did I get you? Who gave you to me?

(He leaves the room.)

ANNETTE *(After a little while)*: Hey! Come back here!

(He returns.)

LEWIS *(Laughing)*: Oh! Christ! You've got me! *(He kisses her)* Oh yes oh yes. Am I a good toy? Do you actually like playing with me? *(She doesn't answer)* You know, we're all alone here. I could kill you now, if I wanted to. I could strangle you, or cut your throat, slip up your neck, like a mouse's neck. *(Pause)* Is that you down there? Hey— who the fuck are you, some half-cooked piece of shit? *(He screams)* Hey—get away from me—you're urine! *(He screams)* You're shit! You're a piece of shit! *(He grabs some food and starts to eat it)* Give me that.

ANNETTE: Lewis, I want you on top of me. I want to be pressed down—very far. I want to go down to the bottom. It's not so far—it's pretty close. All the way down. *(Pause)* Press on me. Press. It's fast. Cold. *(Silence)* Well, do you feel like cheering up?

LEWIS: No.

ANNETTE: Okay. *(Pause)* I'm not tired. *(She hits him. They fight)* Oh—you hurt me. Goddamn you. Goddamn you.

(He sleeps. Pause.)

(To herself) I'm playing. I can climb the gates. And there are piles of grass and hay, on the other side. I know how to roll in it with my friends. *(Pause)* Do you like being kissed there?

(She goes out. Lewis wakes up. She returns with cold cereal, which they prepare and eat.)

This isn't my house. This isn't my home. I really don't like it here. *(Pause)* Why don't you get me out of this?

LEWIS: You could eat the poison.

ANNETTE: But what about you then?

LEWIS: You could get me, too. Just get my face with the knife. Get me a few times.

ANNETTE: If we died, our friends would meet us after, with lots of fruits—pears and apples . . .

LEWIS: Maybe. *(Pause)* Is that what you want? Those pears and apples?

ANNETTE: Yeah.

LEWIS: Well why don't you go get them then?

ANNETTE: I'm afraid.

LEWIS: I'll feed it to you.

(A silence.)

ANNETTE: Then what do you want?

LEWIS: Oh, I want to have lots of children, honey. That's what I want.

(A silence.)

ANNETTE: Lewis—let me go to bed.

LEWIS: I'm not stopping you.

(They freeze. Lights down. Lights up, and Annette is asleep and Lewis awake. Lights down. Lights up again, and Lewis is asleep, and Annette awake. Lights down again. Lights up, and Annette is asleep, Lewis awake. And so on, ad-lib, until the final blackout.)

END

A Thought
in Three Parts

A Thought in Three Parts was first performed in workshop form as *Three Short Plays* in New York in 1976 at the New York Shakespeare Festival/The Public Theater (Joseph Papp, producer). The directors were Wilford Leach (*Summer Evening*) and Leonardo Shapiro (*The Youth Hostel*), music was composed by William Elliot; the production stage manager was Kitzi Becker and the stage manager was Jason La Padura. The cast was:

Summer Evening

DAVID	John Bottoms
SARAH	Deborah Rush

The Youth Hostel

DICK	Jeffrey Horowitz
HELEN	Karen Ludwig
JUDY	Kathleen Tolan
BOB	Colin Garrey
TOM	Ron Van Lieu

Mr. Frivolous

MR. FRIVOLOUS	Frederick Neumann

A Thought in Three Parts was performed in London by the Joint Stock Theatre Group (Max Stafford-Clark, William Gaskill, David Hare, artistic directors) in London on February 28, 1977. It was directed by Max Stafford-Clark; sets were designed by Sue Plummer and lighting was designed by Steven Whitson. The cast was:

Summer Evening

DAVID	Philip Sayer
SARAH	Robyn Goodman

The Youth Hostel

DICK	Jack Klaff
HELEN	Stephanie Fayerman
JUDY	Robyn Goodman
BOB	Paul-John Geoffrey
TOM	Philip Sayer

Mr. Frivolous

MR. FRIVOLOUS	Tony Rohr

A Thought in Three Parts received its U.S. premiere in May 2007 by Rubber Repertory in Austin, Texas, in a production co-produced by Rubber Rep and Vortex Repertory Company. This production was later performed in Marfa, Texas, in a co-production by Rubber Rep and the Goode Crowley Theater. It was directed by Carlos Treviño, Matt Hislope and Josh Meyer; set design was by Chase Staggs, costumes were designed by Brigette Hutchison, lighting was designed by Steve Shirey and sound was designed by Josh Meyer. The cast was:

Summer Evening

DAVID	Mark Stewart
SARAH	Adriene Mishler

The Youth Hostel

DICK	Josh Meyer
HELEN	Rosaruby Glaberman
JUDY	Kelli Bland
BOB	Matt Hislope
TOM	Steven Laing

Mr. Frivolous

MR. FRIVOLOUS	David Yeakle

Summer Evening

A pleasant hotel room in a foreign country. David and Sarah, a couple in their late twenties. A bed by the window, a night table next to it. Sarah is in the bathroom, offstage, at the start. David and Sarah often speak very fast, perhaps much faster than people really speak. Sometimes their dialogue is almost overlapping.

DAVID: Well dinner was not so bad, in fact. Sarah certainly enjoyed her fish a great deal, which I must say I did think was quite a bit better than my rabbit, somehow. You know, rabbit's all right, but actually what with scraping the gravy off with a spoon to try to see the damned thing so that one could try to take out those tiny little bones, I'm not at all sure I wouldn't have done just as well ordering the duck, frankly. Because one couldn't call it filling, and now I'm hungry again, and I'd like to go down and get something to eat. You know, my friends at home quite like me. My friends at home really do. I'm known as a nice—as a good chap, actually. They find me appealing. But we're traveling

35

here. *(Into the bathroom)* Sarah? Sarah?—are you feeling
at all like some—?—

SARAH *(From inside)*: What?

DAVID: —I was thinking—

SARAH *(From inside)*: Just trying things on—

DAVID: —I just thought that we might go down to the—

(Sarah enters.)

SARAH: What?

DAVID: —to the restaurant and—lovely dress, love—the—

SARAH: Well? Don't you think?—just our chocolates, maybe?
Do we really—

DAVID: Well—it might be nice—some sort of a soup, or one
of those—

SARAH: Well—I'd rather—my skirt's ripped—

DAVID: Oh really, darling? I was only thinking that maybe we
could get—we could get some toast—

SARAH: Well then why not go down—

DAVID: I—

SARAH: You probably—

DAVID: —what?

SARAH: You could still—

DAVID: I know, but—

SARAH: I—

DAVID: You come, too. We could just have some toast and tea
and then we could—

SARAH: Well—why not bring something up?

DAVID: —but you don't feel—

SARAH: What?

DAVID: From there? Do you really—

SARAH: I don't—

DAVID: All right, I will, but shouldn't—

SARAH: All right.

DAVID: If you're sure that you—
SARAH: Fine.

(David exits.)

Actually, I really would like some toast. I'll tell you frankly I really like toast a lot. I mean, toast with butter, toast and butter with different kinds of eggs: I like toast with fried eggs; I like toast with poached eggs; and buttered toast and *scrambled* eggs—now that's really marvelous. Especially with orange juice, orange juice with ice. I like jam also, like *all* breakfast foods. *(Pause)* I must say sometimes I rather would like to lie in bed all day and all night and just have tea and toast and jam, if a maid would bring them, I mean. I rather would like to solve little puzzles, and do little drawings, and write little plays to read to myself. And I rather would like to lie there in bed with my feet just quietly touching each other, and if a crumb of toast by chance would happen to fall onto the sheets and find its way down to the bottom of the bed, I wouldn't mind. I wouldn't mind occasionally spilling my tea, if it wasn't too hot, or even spilling a cold drink maybe, you know, just spilling these different drinks in my bed and dropping some toast in my bed as well. Now I know that butter is hard to clean off of one's sheets, and toast is hard to clean out of one's bed, and tea and drinks could stain the sheets too, but it might be nice just to have them there, just to have them with me under the sheets. And I think I might like to splash around quite a bit with that mess in my bed, and kick my legs a bit in my bed, and rub my bottom into my bed. And if I needed to pee I would pee in my bed, and my feet would get pretty wet in my bed. *(Pause)* That's the way I would like it to be when

I could read then too—read all sorts of books and newspapers that I would enjoy. I would keep getting new ones and keep a big basket right near me to throw the old newspapers in and even the old books in. It would need to get dumped out sometimes, and I'd dump it right onto the floor, and then I'd kick it about quite a bit. I would rather enjoy to have a sandwich or two in there too to kick about on the floor, and then have some bits of things on my feet as I climbed back in bed and took out my book and tasted my tea and spilled a bit more in the bed. And in the book I would read about people at a table having tea and toast, with plates and napkins and glass which sparkles and cuts and shines, and the women wearing dresses with red and white jewels, where red and white jewels would be stuck on the clothes.

(David returns with a tray of fruit and other things.)

DAVID: Now darling, I—
SARAH: What?
DAVID: —wasn't able to get what you—
SARAH: What did you get?
DAVID: These are not what we—
SARAH: Oh—well I really don't mind. They seem fine.
DAVID: Well, do they, darling? I'd wanted—
SARAH: They're fine.
DAVID: Oh, I—
SARAH: Yes, they're— *(Silence. They eat. As they eat)* Yes I'm quite content, love—
DAVID: I'm glad, my darling—are you happy, with? —
SARAH: —how they *find* fruit so ripe—
DAVID: I—

SARAH: —the napkins, and look—

DAVID: —and just always be happy—

SARAH: —these toothpicks—

DAVID: —and—

SARAH: —start sort of flat, and then get round, and then come to a point—

DAVID: Your teeth are so pretty—the way you bite those things—

SARAH: Do you like my teeth, love? —These saucers—I wish we—

DAVID: I—

SARAH: Wait, though! You still haven't seen my—

(She goes into the bathroom and shuts the door.)

DAVID: Quietly I watch her dress, undress. Incredible, incredible, she has no idea the trembling in my heart as I lie in bed and watch her clothing, falling to the floor, softly to the chair.

(Sarah enters in a new dress.)

My God—did you get this dress—today? Your breasts—

SARAH: I—yes—

DAVID: —they—

SARAH: I was thinking—

DAVID: —that color—

SARAH: —this top with the very same dress—it seems almost too thin, but I like the sleeves—

DAVID: —lie down for a bit? —

(They lie down on the bed. Silence.)

You know, there was dancing downstairs—I was really amazed—

SARAH: There was?

DAVID: —the way they—

SARAH: Now darling—

DAVID: Don't you find it amazing?

SARAH: Yes.

DAVID: —the way their elbows—those angles—

SARAH: Yes?—

DAVID: And I love that strange music—

SARAH: Yes—

DAVID: —that sort of drunken, that crippled—step—

SARAH: Yes—

DAVID: Oh my love—

SARAH: Am I your love, darling?

DAVID: Oh yes, my love. My love. My love. What? Do you loathe me?

SARAH: No.

DAVID: But you're feeling—?—

SARAH: What?

DAVID: —in some—way—?—

SARAH: Why? What? Am I—?—

DAVID: No, but you—

SARAH: What?

DAVID: Would you like that other pear, my love?

(She doesn't reply. He doesn't move.)

No? Well then, darling, I think I'll read. *(Pause)* But you're feeling quite happy?

SARAH: Thank you.

DAVID: You just enjoy thinking? Well, I'll just read quietly, and you can think.

SARAH: I'm— *(Pause)*

DAVID: Thinking tragic thoughts, darling?—

SARAH: I'm not thinking, actually.

DAVID: No—well I didn't—

SARAH: I'm not thinking, actually.

DAVID: I didn't—

SARAH: What?

DAVID: —that you *had* to be thinking—

SARAH: Well no. Yes. But I wonder if you do mind terribly my looking out the window? Does it stop you from reading?

DAVID: Not at all, my love—I was only hoping your thoughts weren't tragic—

SARAH: Yes.

DAVID: And now I'm glad that they aren't, my love. *(Silence)* Yes, it's amazing how *in*expensive the fruit was, in fact, and I really thought it was awfully good. —Didn't you?

SARAH: Yes.

DAVID: This hotel isn't bad—

SARAH: It—no—

DAVID: And the other one really wasn't much less expensive.

SARAH: Well no—not really.

DAVID: You mean, you think it was actually quite a bit less expensive, in fact?

SARAH: Well no, I meant you were right, it wasn't much less expensive at all, actually.

(She gets up from the bed.)

DAVID: Well that's what—yes—

(She goes into the bathroom and shuts the door.)

Help me. Help me. I want to be hugged. I want to be bound up. I want to be kissed. Stay with me. Stay with me. Don't stop me. I love you. I—

(She enters in a new dress.)

SARAH: This one I got—

DAVID: —that's marvelous, actually—

SARAH: —*inexpensively*, and—

DAVID: Very nice *indeed*—

SARAH: —*incredibly* cheap—yes I will have that pear—do you want—

DAVID: No, no—your legs—so lovely, my darling, so perfect—

SARAH: Oo—just delicious—so sweet—

DAVID: —take the tray out into the hall, I think—I'm afraid of the bugs—

(He exits.)

SARAH: It's strange, there's nothing, there isn't anything I wouldn't, I wouldn't, I wouldn't do for pleasure. I'd stick a hot poker up my ass if I thought I would like it.

(David enters.)

DAVID: I love you. I love you.

SARAH: —look cute in that funny-looking shirt, my love— *(She turns up her collar)* —do you like it like this?

DAVID: Oh yes. Oh yes. Oh yes. It's appealing.

SARAH: Oh, do you find me appealing?

DAVID: I find you—

SARAH: Thank you—

DAVID: —maybe with a scarf?— *(Silence. He sits in a chair)* There are so many sounds out there, aren't there?— things in the trees—and that constant *bang*—

SARAH: —a festival there by the sea, my love—

DAVID: —a what?—

SARAH: —they're dancing and singing and selling those—

DAVID: —what?—selling?—

SARAH: —those things that they make—with straw, those paper—

DAVID: You mean those hats?—
SARAH: Oh, they're from a different—
DAVID: Oh, are they?
SARAH: These are—
DAVID: I thought they—
SARAH: These are those things made of twigs, the faces—
DAVID: Oh God, those prune-faced—
SARAH: They've got all the fruit out too—a regular market—oh, darling, we—
DAVID: I was wondering—

(Silence.)

SARAH: Do you like it better buttoned to the top?
DAVID: Let me see it without the—
SARAH: Like this?
DAVID: That's nice. I like it.
SARAH: Or this?
DAVID: So nice. *(Silence)* Do you want to lie down?
SARAH: Why not?
DAVID: Then let's.

(They lie down on the bed. She takes a box of chocolates from the night table.)

SARAH. A chocolate?
DAVID: No thank you.
SARAH: Pardon me. I will. *(She eats one, then puts them away)* I'll just read slightly.
DAVID: Oh, read? Read. That's good. That's good.

(Silence. They read. She slams her book shut.)

Oh, what's wrong, darling?

43

SARAH: I'm sorry.

DAVID: No, love. No no. That's fine. I'm happy reading here.

SARAH: Well I'm not so happy. I don't like this book. I hate it. I'm sorry.

DAVID: —don't like it?—

SARAH: —not funny, it's dirty—I hate it.

DAVID: I'm sorry.

SARAH: Well it's not your fault—

DAVID: Well it is, I'm sure.

SARAH: Well I really don't think so—

DAVID: I think—

SARAH: What?

DAVID: No—you know—well—I feel—would you like to play cards?

SARAH: No—

DAVID: A short game?—

SARAH: No thank you—

DAVID: I'm only—

SARAH: Yes.

DAVID: —trying—

SARAH: I'm quite—

DAVID: I'm just trying to think now—I'm trying—

SARAH: I'm very, very sorry.

DAVID: No, *I'm* sorry—I'm just trying to think—are there any other sorts of games with the cards that we haven't ever tried—

SARAH: I'm very, very sorry.

DAVID: Well don't—

SARAH: What?

DAVID: I'm only—

SARAH: You what?

DAVID: —feel perhaps we might just try to sleep?

SARAH: I'm not tired. I'm not tired. I'm not tired.

DAVID: Well—you mean—

SARAH: I can't sleep now.

DAVID: Well, I thought you looked sleepy—but do you mean you can't sleep because you're afraid of the—?—

SARAH: What? No! Do you mean those bugs?

DAVID: No—no—I just meant that I really wouldn't think that those bugs are actually really a danger—they're only—

SARAH: Oh no? Well all right, then—you're apparently an expert in—

DAVID: I'm not saying that, but I think that we probably might have been warned if—it's not awfully likely that *we* were the only ones ever to see—you're not sleepy at all? Well, that could be because of course you *did* take—

SARAH: But you sleep. *I* just can't. I'm sorry. I'm hot. I'm sorry. I'm sorry.

DAVID: Yes. Yes, I was afraid that maybe if you *did* take a nap this afternoon—

SARAH: You what?

DAVID: Well, you know, often a nap—

SARAH: The what?—can't *you* sleep? *I'm* all right. *I'm*—

DAVID: And you don't want to read?

SARAH: Because I just like to sit here and watch all the people, actually.

DAVID: Well yes, but that's fine, and I mean we could both make a trip down there right now and come back. And I'd really rather like—

SARAH: Well, in fact, you see, I could take a quick trip down there by myself—

DAVID: But then why don't we go? I'll just change my shirt— *(He gets up from the bed and starts to change)* And I know *you* won't mind if it rains, my love—

SARAH: The—

DAVID: And if our shoes *do* get wet, then we still have those—

SARAH: David—

DAVID: —those sandals—

SARAH: I—

DAVID: Yes, I *have* been wondering whether actually we *should* have stayed here. You know? Really? It *is so expensive*, and you're right that the heat in these rooms—

SARAH: Well, but how could you know that you wouldn't in fact have got something worse at the other one, actually?

DAVID: Well—

SARAH: I mean at least here the bathroom—

DAVID: —the bathroom is *great*—I mean, better than—

SARAH: —Yes, well *I* think it's nice—

DAVID: Well, I'm ready. All right?

SARAH: David—

DAVID: What?

SARAH: I can't. Please. Really. Please. No please don't touch me. Please. No. Really. Don't.

(Silence.)

DAVID: Yes. Well. Fine. You see, I actually had thought, in some way—

(Silence. He returns to the bed.)

SARAH: Yes. Well I guess you're right. We paid a great deal—

DAVID: We what?

SARAH: We paid a great deal, we really paid a great deal for this room, which I'd call a pretty ugly little room, I should say—

DAVID: You don't find it attractive?

SARAH: No I wouldn't say I do.

DAVID: Well—it may not be.

SARAH: Well—it isn't.

DAVID: Well—it might not be. Though I rather like it. You see, I rather like it, myself, in fact.

SARAH: Oh, really? Well I rather hate it, myself, you see—

DAVID: —you—

SARAH: Because I don't really like our little lamp very much, and I don't really like our little table very much. And I rather think that that rug there is ugly. And I rather think that that other rug is ugly. And I rather think that that other rug is ugly. And I rather think that that other rug is ugly. And I rather think that that other rug is ugly. And I wonder—do you like these blankets, David?

DAVID: Well—yes I do, actually.

SARAH: Well I don't think I like them, you see. I mean this design is all right—but the way they feel—

DAVID: —the material, you find?—

SARAH: I don't really like this material—no—

DAVID: You find it unpleasant, or somehow—?—

SARAH: Yes, it's—oh my God, this picture just came into my mind, I thought of you strangling me—

DAVID: Yes? Some sort of a fantasy?

SARAH: I've actually never imagined the feeling of choking. One might get quite queasy—

DAVID: Well—

SARAH: —dizzy—

DAVID: Yes, they say that you—

SARAH: But why not hug me, David? You know how to hug me, don't you?—

DAVID: Would you like to put your head on my chest?

SARAH: Just—there—

DAVID: Quite pleasant—but are some of your bones—?— er—

SARAH: No—not really—

DAVID: I feel that your head—

SARAH: No—no, don't move it. That's fine. *(Silence)* Am I stopping you from reading now, David? Am I?

DAVID: No. Not really. No, I wouldn't say so.

SARAH: Good. I'm only trying to lie here, darling. Not to harm you. Not to destroy you.

DAVID: Good. Good.

SARAH: —don't want to destroy you. *Will* you kill me, David?

DAVID: No, my love. No, my sweet. You know I won't kill you. I'll always protect you. Just always protect you.

SARAH: I mean, these feelings—these feelings—of love and love and love and love—

DAVID: Do you love me, my darling?

SARAH: Well, do you know what feelings of love really actually are? Do you know what love means?

DAVID: Well—

SARAH: Or are you actually only a little piece of shit who's learned how to *talk* about feelings?

DAVID: I don't *think* that I—

SARAH: How can you tell?

DAVID: Well I can't be *sure*—

SARAH: Do you know what love means?

DAVID: You know, I can't be *sure*—

SARAH: You can't what?

DAVID: —that I know—

SARAH: You can't?

DAVID: What? Do you want me to lie? Is that what you want?

SARAH: Well I think that I do.

DAVID: Well then, certainly, yes, I definitely know.

SARAH: Well that's fine then. You know what it means.

DAVID: I certainly do.

SARAH: Well I wish that I did.

DAVID: I'm sorry.

SARAH: I wish that I did.

DAVID: I'm very sorry.

SARAH: Can you tell me something about it?

DAVID: Sure. Of course. It's quite like hatred—

SARAH: Yes—

DAVID: An intense focus on the other person.

SARAH: Thanks. That's helpful. I think that you're really on to it there.

DAVID: Thank you. Really.

SARAH: I once put a silver coin on my tongue. Do you know? I dried up, then I was dripping with sweat. My lips were stiff—yes, the coin was an eye. I was watching the ocean. The water was black. I was barefoot. The sun stood by me, it was tiny, it was white, it was burning the water. The water was twisting in pain. It was crying.

DAVID: And you felt—a sticky feeling?

SARAH: —yes—

DAVID: A drippy feeling?

SARAH: —yes—

DAVID: Now here's what I picture. There's a big spotted field, and you're lying there dead. It's night, there are stars, there are clouds, and they're racing in the sky, and I'm dragging your body by the feet, dirty feet. Your head gets bloody. I'm running fast. At the end there's a stream, and I lay you down into it and wash you. I stretch you out under a tree, on the grass. I try to kiss you, but you're dry and sour. Maybe I'll burn you.

SARAH: David?

DAVID: Yes?

SARAH: Will you leave me tonight, darling?

DAVID: Tonight? What? Will I leave you *tonight*? Here's a book I don't feel like reading. Here's one I don't feel like. Here's one I don't think that I—God, do you hear those sounds? They never get tired.

SARAH: No.

DAVID: But we're always tired. Aren't we, Sarah?

SARAH: Oh no. I don't think so.

(She touches him. Pause.)

DAVID: Maybe tomorrow we should buy that dress—the white one with the flowers? *(Pause)*

SARAH: —yes—maybe—

DAVID: But don't you like it?

SARAH: Oh, I do, yes—

DAVID: I loved those red flowers with those very pale leaves—

(He kisses her. She turns a switch on the night table, and the lights of the room go out. Light still comes in from outside. They touch.)

SARAH: Oh my God, yes.

(Blackout.)

THE YOUTH HOSTEL

Two sparsely furnished rooms, not connected, dimly lit, with no windows. Room 1, stage left; Room 2, stage right. Room 1, Dick sitting on the bed, thinking. Room 2, empty. Sounds of birds outside. Long silence before Dick speaks.

DICK: Well—seem to be alone here. Nobody else in. Birds singin' outside. Nothin' much to do—just sit around I guess.

(Pause. Room 2, Judy enters. She turns down the bed, neatens the room, as the scene in Room 1 progresses.)

Fun to play with toys, but don't got none. *(Helen enters Room 1)* What? Oh hi, Helen.
HELEN: Hi, Dick.
DICK: Aren't you out with the others?
HELEN: Nope. Guess not. *(Pause)* I guess I'm just different— like you, Dick.
DICK: Yeah, I guess so, Helen. *(Pause)*

HELEN: Mind if I sit down? I'm feelin' a bit ill.

DICK: Why not. Go ahead. *(She sits down)*

HELEN: Yeah. My stomach's been gettin' to me. Makin' me sick. I hate bein' sick—y'know?

DICK: Yeah.

(Pause.)

HELEN: Can you guess what I was doing just before I came in here, Dick?

DICK: No. What?

HELEN: I was doing fuckin' nothing.

DICK: Yeah. That's too bad. *(Pause)* I hope you're in a good mood now, though, Helen.

HELEN: Well I hope you are, Dick.

DICK: Well, I might be.

HELEN: You stupid asshole.

DICK: Yeah.

HELEN: You stupid asshole.

(Room 2. A knock at the door.)

JUDY: Yes—who is it?

BOB *(Outside)*: Well— It's me—Bob—

JUDY: Oh— *(Pause)* —Hi, Bob!

BOB *(Outside)*: May I come in?

JUDY: Oh— *(Pause)* —sure! *(Bob enters)* Gee, Bob—you look all upset. *(Pause)* What's wrong?

BOB: I don't know, Judy. I guess I just can't sleep.

JUDY: Can't sleep? Gosh—why, Bob? Are you—too upset?

BOB: No—not exactly. I can't quite explain.

JUDY: You can't? *(Pause)*

BOB: You see—I'm too nervous to sleep. I'm just too disturbed—

JUDY: Gosh, Bob—

BOB: Can I sit down at least?

JUDY: Of course—I didn't mean— *(He sits down)*

BOB: You see, I've never had a girlfriend, Judy, and— *(Pause)*

JUDY: I see—you're afraid you just don't know how to talk to girls.

BOB: Yes.

JUDY: Well— *(Pause)* —I think you're doing just fine right now . . .

BOB: Gee—thanks, Judy. You're the kind of girl a fella might really like to talk to. Really.

JUDY: Well, thank you, Bob.

BOB: No—I mean it.

JUDY: That's nice, Bob. I really appreciate it.

(Very long silence.)

BOB: Judy—Judy—you know how bad I'd like to touch you.

JUDY: Oh now, Bob—don't frighten me like that.

BOB: No, I don't mean to frighten you. But I want so bad just only to look at you—

JUDY: Only to look, Bob?

BOB: I want to see your breasts, Judy.

JUDY: What—you mean—naked, Bob?

BOB: Yes, Judy. I need to. Really. I won't touch you. I promise. I promise. But I just can't sleep. I can't leave this room. I won't look hard, Judy. But just to look.

JUDY: Bob—I don't know you—

BOB: You have to, Judy. I just can't leave.

(She sits silently for a long while on her bed. Then she takes off her shirt.)

Thank you, Judy.

JUDY: Will you leave now, Bob?

BOB: No—I need more, Judy. Your pants too.

JUDY: Oh Bob—please—

BOB: No—I really need it, Judy. I have to see it.

(She slowly takes off her pants. Nude, she sits on the bed so that he can see her genitals. She looks sad. He looks at her carefully from his chair.)

Thank you, Judy. Should I touch it?

JUDY: No, Bob.

(He stands. Stripping, he approaches her. Then he slowly penetrates her and makes love to her until he comes.)

BOB: It's not enough, Judy.

JUDY: No. *(He goes back to his chair)*

BOB: I expected more.

JUDY: I know.

BOB: Why do you hate me?

JUDY: I don't hate you, Bob.

BOB: I want more.

JUDY: Bob, really—

BOB: Let's get married, Judy.

JUDY: No, Bob. Put on your pants. You'll catch cold.

BOB: Thanks, Judy. *(He picks up his pants, but doesn't put them on)* I hate you. But I love you, Judy.

JUDY: I know, Bob. I'm very cold. I'm going to get dressed. *(She puts on her shirt)*

BOB: Thank you, Judy.

JUDY: Let's try to stop now.

BOB: I know, Judy.

JUDY: I'd rather go to bed now. I'd like to sleep.

BOB: I know, Judy.

JUDY: Don't you want to leave now, Bob?

BOB: No, not really—I'll just stay here. I think we'll fall asleep soon.

JUDY: I know, Bob—but don't you think you should leave? I'd like to masturbate.

BOB: I'll watch you, Judy.

JUDY: No, Bob, I could never do it then.

BOB: Get onto the side of the bed, and I'll get on this side, and we'll both do it, and we won't see each other.

JUDY: All right, Bob. We'll see who comes first.

BOB: I'm sure you will, Judy.

(They go to opposite sides of the bed and both masturbate. She comes first.)

JUDY: That was wonderful. Are you coming, Bob?

BOB: Not yet—now shut up.

JUDY: All right, Bob. I feel terrific—really exhilarated. Gee whiz. Oh come on, Bob—you sure are slow.

BOB: Oh—oh—that helped me! *(He comes)* Get me some tissues, Judy. I feel like a fool.

JUDY: All right, Bob. Here. Ugh—what a mess.

BOB: Gee thanks, Judy. Give me a kiss. Here—right here. *(He points to his cheek. She kisses it)* Thanks, Judy. I guess I'd better go. I hate myself—but I'd like to sleep somewhere else.

JUDY: That's fine, Bob. I'm going to jerk off some more. So get your ass out.

BOB: Don't be vulgar, Judy.

JUDY: I'm not, Bob. I just love to jerk off.

(Bob leaves. She lies on the bed and masturbates.)

I really love this. It turns me on. There! Ah! Mmm . . .

(Long silence. She lies in bed, but doesn't sleep. In Room 1, Helen is wandering around the room. Dick is sitting in a chair.)

HELEN *(Playing with flowers)*: I like flowers.
DICK: Yeah?
HELEN: They're really attractive.
DICK: Are they?
HELEN: Yeah. I sometimes feel they're really great.
DICK: Yeah.
HELEN: Why don't we get a few more? Really decorate the place.
DICK: Yeah. Why not?

(Pause.)

HELEN: I feel so lonely, Dick. Would you like to hug me for a minute?
DICK: Well I really don't want to, Helen.
HELEN: No?
DICK: Fuckin' sorry, but I'm feelin' sort of sick.
HELEN: Yeah. I'll fuckin' hug myself.

(She climbs onto the bed, gets under the covers, and throws her pants out onto the floor. She touches herself under the covers.)

DICK: You really make me sick, Helen. You really do. I really hate you.
HELEN: Really, Dick?
DICK: You're not the kind of person I like now, Helen.
HELEN: Oh, aren't I, Dick?
DICK: No. You really aren't.
HELEN: Well what sort of person do you like now then, Dickie? Why don't you tell me? I'm really interested.
DICK: Well, people more like Joan, Helen—or people like Alice.

HELEN: Alice? Really? Is she the one you like, Dick? I'll bet she is.

DICK: Well—I do like her, Helen.

HELEN: Yeah—she's really your type. She's really your type, Dick.

DICK: You dripping cunt—will you leave me alone?

HELEN: She's really your type, Dick. Just the type you wet your pants for. Should I tell you all about her, Dickie?

DICK: No.

HELEN: I'll just tell you a few things. I think you'll find them fascinating.

DICK: Go eat yourself, Helen.

HELEN: To start with, sweetheart, her asshole is covered with shit. She's never used toilet paper in her fuckin' life. She's got dirt on her arms up to her elbows. And she's a fuckin' liar, and she stole my razor blades twice in a row, and then she fuckin' hid them. —Do you want to hear more of this?

DICK: Go on—why not? What the hell do I care?

HELEN: She eats shit in her room. Wendy watched her. It's not even secret. She'll never do it for me because she knows I hate her, but she does it in front of everybody, all the time. She hasn't shaved her body once since the day she was born, so she looks like a big hairy tree, with big black roots running into the ground. I once tripped her up and stripped off her shirt just to look at her. She looked like a dirty, filthy pig. I pulled down her under-wear to look at her crotch, and I was almost sick. It was like a stinking forest growing in all directions. I wanted to look, but she tried to stop me. She stuck her fist in my eye. She almost blinded me. She could have killed me. I tried to smash her head on the ground, but she hit me in the nose, and I was bleeding all over.

DICK: That's great, Helen.

HELEN: Why do you like her so much? Why? Why? Why don't you tell me?

DICK: I don't know. I think she's a decent person. She seems like a good person, like a good person. She's a person, a decent—a person, a person, a decent—I like her. I don't see why you don't like her.

HELEN: Have you ever eaten a meal with her?

DICK: A thousand times. I've always liked it. She's a pleasant companion.

HELEN: Did you watch her eat?

DICK: What do you mean did I watch her eat?

HELEN: I mean, did you watch her eat?

DICK: But what do you mean did I watch her eat? What do you mean did I watch her eat?

HELEN: I mean, did you watch her eat?

DICK: I don't know what you mean.

HELEN: I mean, did you watch her eat, Dick? Did you watch her eat?

DICK: I don't know what you want me to say. I don't know what you want. I don't know what you want. You want me to say things, Helen. What do you want? I don't get it. I don't get it.

HELEN: I said, did you ever watch her when she eats? She doesn't eat the way I think you mean I think I think, Dick. *Now* stop me.

DICK: I'll stop you, Helen, and I really mean it, so you better listen. Now, Alice is my friend. A fine person. I want to know her. I do *not* want to discuss these things, to fight, to argue. We're talking here about my friend Alice, and if you don't like her you can go and drown yourself in shit for all I care, but I don't want to hear these insults and lies. I want the truth.

HELEN: Oh do you, Dickie? You want the truth?

DICK: Yes.

HELEN: You want the truth? Well here it is—your great friend Alice is hated by everyone, including me, and she knows it. Consequently she's taking revenge by making herself disgusting to everybody, and she's leading you off to be a friend of hers so she can make you just like her. She'll catch you off your guard, and you'll be eating shit, too, Dickie—just like Alice.

DICK: Well well.

HELEN: Yes—that's the truth, baby Dickie. So like it, honey. I hope you like it. *(Pause)*

DICK: You really get to me, Helen. You really do.

(Long pause. In Room 2, Judy gets out of bed, puts on a skirt, and sits in a chair.)

HELEN: I wish I were dead.

DICK: Is that right? Why is that, Helen?

HELEN: Go fuck yourself, Dick.

DICK: Gee thanks, Helen.

HELEN: "Gee thanks, Helen." You really are an asshole, Dickie.

DICK: Yeah, thanks. Thanks a lot, sweetheart. Why don't you leave me alone?

HELEN: Well why the hell should I?

DICK: Because I want you to. I'm sick of you.

HELEN: Really? Really? *(She lifts up the bed covers)* Are you sick of this?

DICK: Oh come on, Helen.

HELEN: Come on, Dick. Just finger me, Dickie.

DICK: Why the hell should I?

HELEN: Well why don't you, Dick? Please? Please?

DICK: You're just sitting there, Helen! *(He goes to the bed and fingers her)* I'll feel your asshole too.

HELEN: Oh God.

DICK: Is that okay?

HELEN: Okay! Okay! Oh! *(She comes. Pause)*

DICK: Yeah—well—look what you've done to my fingers. God!

HELEN: Well—so what?

DICK: Yeah—so what for you. *(Wiping his fingers)* You've fuckin' wrecked my whole fuckin' day, Goddamn fuckin' shit—

HELEN: Yeah—well—thanks, Dick.

DICK: Yeah—thanks for nothing. Get out of here.

HELEN: Yeah, okay, Dickie. See you around.

DICK: Yeah. So long, Helen.

HELEN: So long, Dick. *(She exits)*

DICK: Yeah. Well. I'm sick to death of these pushy people. What's the point? Do I need that? I'm going to lie right down here and jerk myself off, and if anybody tries to stop me it's their tough luck. That's my fuckin' point of view.

(He lies down and begins to masturbate. Judy leaves Room 2 and enters Room 1.)

JUDY: Oh, hi, Dick! Are you jerking off?

DICK: Well—I *was*. I'm gonna go nuts!

JUDY: But what's the matter? Don't you feel like talking? I thought you'd be lonely.

DICK: Oh Judy—I've been trying to be by myself for hours. Helen's been in here giving me a hard time.

JUDY: Oh—really? Here—let me do it. *(She starts to jerk him off)*

DICK: No—really—Judy—you really don't need to.

JUDY: I want to—honestly, Dickie.

DICK: I know, Judy, but—

JUDY: You don't want me to? Do you want to have me?

DICK: No—I only—

JUDY *(Pulling up her skirt)*: Look—here—here—let me get right on you. Oh—oh—you see?—wowee— *(She sits on him, and they make love)* Oh, boy—this is really enjoyable! Yes! Yes!

(She comes, then he immediately comes.)

Oh, gee—

DICK: Yeah—I have to admit that felt awfully good, Judy. I'm glad you did it to me.

JUDY: Thanks, Dick.

DICK: You've really got a good, sticky hole. It's really a good one.

JUDY: I like you too, Dick.

DICK: But why aren't you out with the others, though, Judy?

JUDY: 'Cause I'm in here fuckin' you, Dick. Now, you know that.

DICK: No, but I mean—

JUDY: No but *I* mean I came here on purpose to fuck you.

DICK: What? You did? But why, Judy? Do you like me that much?

JUDY: Well—do you really want to know how much?

DICK: Well—how much, Judy?

JUDY: I love you, Dickie!

DICK: Really? You do? But what do you mean?

JUDY: From the first time I saw you. You looked really special to me. Different! Really!

DICK: Why, Judy! I'm amazed!—Of course I always liked you too, Judy—in those cute little shorts—you could almost see your vagina—and those downy hairs on your thighs—

JUDY: I knew you loved those shorts, Dick. I only wore them 'cause I knew you loved them.

DICK: God—and to think I didn't know—never even thought you felt anything about me. And here we are! Gosh—isn't it great?

JUDY: Yeah—it really is. Oh God—let's do it some more.

(They make love again and both come. They lie quietly. Long silence.)

DICK: Judy?

JUDY: Yes?

DICK: You have a beautiful body. I've never see tits like that—they're so small and petite.

JUDY: I know, Dick.

DICK: I just love everything about you.

(Pause.)

It's dark in here.

JUDY: Yeah.

DICK: You know, there used to be a bear that lived over there. You see?—that spot was some of his urine.

JUDY: Gee, Dick—

DICK: You see, there was a forest over there, and a big red house . . .

JUDY: Gosh, Dick—

DICK: But you'd better go away now, Judy, though, really. *(Pause)* I'm beginning to get that feeling—you know?

JUDY: What do you mean, Dick? What feeling?

DICK: I'm beginning to wonder what I like about you, Judy. I'm beginning to feel a bit strange—and I don't think I want you here anymore—I'm beginning to wonder if you're too thin for me, Judy.

JUDY: Dick—I don't understand—

DICK: No—I really mean it, Judy. You're too thin—your ass—please, Judy, please go before I get you now! I'd have to get you, Judy—so get out now!

JUDY: All right! All right!

DICK: You'd better go! You'd better hurry up! Get out! Get out! Now! Now! *(Judy exits, leaving her skirt behind)* I'm mortified. I kicked her out as if she were a dog. But what could I do? I hated her! She's too thin! She's just not healthy! When I saw that ass, like a pushed-in face— No! No! I really could have killed her! My God! My God! And she was so good-looking—that wonderful vagina, those breasts—so tiny! I loved them so much! But I felt too angry. *(Pause)* It's all so hard—it's so *difficult* . . . *(Pause)* Oh God—God—tired's not the word. I need such a rest. A rest, quiet. Lots of swimming. *(He masturbates, making sounds. He comes, with more sounds)* Ah—that was great. Good orgasm! God—I really needed it. *(Pause)* Wow. Good. Now I'll sleep . . .

(He sleeps. Judy enters, looking for her skirt.)

JUDY: I'm sorry, I left my— Hey, he's asleep! *(Pause)* God, he doesn't look so frightening now! Hi, sleepyhead— where'd you put my skirt?

(Helen enters in a skirt and top.)

HELEN: Oh—hello there, Judy.

JUDY: Well—well well well! Hi, Helen!

HELEN: Hi, Judy.

JUDY: Have you come to see Dick? He seems a bit grumpy.

HELEN: I think he's sleeping, Judy.

JUDY: Yeah—well—you know what I mean. *(Pause)*

HELEN: Yes, I've been feeling a bit bored, you know, lately, Judy—

JUDY: Uh-huh—

HELEN: And I thought I might visit a little penis he has, you know?

JUDY: Oh—really? Why not visit mine, Helen?

HELEN: That's very funny, Judy. (*She lifts Dick's blanket and puts her head under it*) Let's see who's here. Hello? Hello? Does he have one in here, somewhere, d'you think? I can't seem to find it. (*Judy lifts up Helen's skirt and puts her head under it. Helen shrieks*) Oh God, that tickles!

(*Helen pulls away, laughing. Judy follows her, laughing wildly. Helen climbs onto the bed to escape. Judy climbs on also. Both are laughing wildly. Dick wakes up with a start.*)

DICK: Hey! What!? What the—

JUDY: Hi there, Dick! Just grabbing a little bite here—

(*She rips Helen's skirt off and starts to kiss her genitals. At first Helen fights her, laughing wildly, but then she relents. Dick watches them.*)

DICK: Hey—how's she doing there, Helen?

HELEN: Well I'm not too sure. (*Pause*) She's really a pig. Ow—come on now, Judy!

DICK: Is she really that bad?

HELEN: Oh really, Judy! Really! Really!

JUDY (*She looks up*): What's wrong, you shit?

DICK: You cunts. How disgusting.

HELEN: You made him grow a penis there, Judy. See?

JUDY: Hey, I think I like that. (*She starts to suck Dick's penis*)

DICK: Hey! (*He starts to laugh loudly*)

HELEN: You like that, huh, Dick.
DICK: She's not bad at this, Helen!

(Dick is laughing wildly. Helen is looking for something.)

HELEN: Where is that fuckin' thing?

(Helen finds a dildo and begins to masturbate with it on the bed, while Dick continues to laugh. Finally he comes. Helen continues masturbating.)

DICK: Not bad, Judy.
JUDY: Hey, look what she's doing.
DICK: Hm . . . Rather delightful.
JUDY: Thinks she's pretty clever, I can certainly see that. *(Helen comes)* Can I borrow it, Helen?
HELEN: Go fuck yourself, Judy.
JUDY: Why not? *(Helen begins to masturbate again with the dildo)* Oh come on, Helen. Why not? *(Helen ignores her)* Why not?
HELEN: It's really something—

(Judy rushes at Helen, as if to grab the dildo, but Dick pushes her away.)

DICK: Get out of here, Judy. Come on, get out.
JUDY *(She yells at them)*: You repulsive shits!

(She goes out, slamming the door. Helen masturbates more and more vigorously. Dick gets out of bed, goes to a big box, takes some food out of it, and eats it. Bob enters.)

DICK: Hey—hi there, Bob.
BOB: Hi, Dick—my God—what she's doing!—

DICK: You like that, Bob?

BOB: You're naked, Helen—I can see your— *(Pause)*

DICK: Do you like that, Bob old man?

BOB: Oh God, gee—I can hardly stand this, Dick. I can really see in there. Every part of her vagina. What she's doing—what she's doing—

(Helen comes, she lies exhausted for a moment, puts down the dildo.)

HELEN: Oh. God. Well hi there, Bob.

BOB: Hi, Helen.

HELEN: Hi. Hi hi.

DICK: Well go ahead, Bob. You want to jerk off, you just go ahead. We won't stop you. *(He returns to the bed)*

HELEN: He wants to jerk off?

DICK: Well, don't you, Bob?

HELEN *(To Bob)*: Yeah, we can't stop you. *(Pause)*

BOB: Really? Really? You mean you want to see it?

DICK: If you want to show it.

BOB *(He takes out his penis)*: See? Look.

DICK: It seems all right.

HELEN: Yeah. It looks like a penis.

(Bob is sitting on the bed with Helen and Dick. He masturbates. Helen and Dick watch.)

BOB *(Masturbating faster and faster)*: I'm coming soon!

DICK: Oh boy—

HELEN: Oh—God—

BOB: Oh! *(He comes, shooting sperm toward Helen and Dick)*

DICK: Whoops—catch!—yuck. *(Helen is laughing hysterically)*

HELEN *(To Bob, laughing)*: You're such an asshole!

BOB: Oh wow—that was good—

HELEN: Yuck! Yuck! What an asshole!

BOB: Well—why not? Can you equal me, Dick?

DICK: Can I what? What?

BOB: Well—can you?

HELEN: Yeah, Dick. Let's have a little contest. Let's see how you do. *(Pointing to either side of her)* Now you should be right there, and you should be right there. And now here's my pretty little belly, and on the next step up are my nice little tits, and all the way up is my cute little neck. Now aim this way, and let's see who gets higher.

DICK: Oh come on, Helen.

BOB: Yeah, let's see it, Dick.

DICK: Are you really serious?

HELEN: Come *on*, Dick! Stop wasting our time.

DICK: Well come on, Helen! I don't think I'm in the mood.

HELEN: I hate him! I hate him! All right, I'll start you. *(She kisses him until he starts to laugh)*

DICK: Okay! Okay!

HELEN: I really hate you, Dick. *(Bob and Dick both start to masturbate)* All right then, come on, boys. Let's see a little speed. Let's go. Let's go!

BOB: I'm closer—oh God—

(Bob comes. Then Dick comes. Silence. Then Helen speaks.)

HELEN: Boy, I'm feeling pretty wet up there, Bob. I'm really soaked.

DICK: Well I thought mine was higher.

HELEN: Oh come off it, Dick.

DICK: Well—wasn't it, Bob?

BOB: Well you did pretty well there, Dick, but I thought mine was up to her face.

DICK: You what?

BOB: Think I'll try it again.

HELEN: Could you aim for my mouth?

BOB: Well there's no harm trying. *(He starts to masturbate)*

HELEN: Well come on then, Dick.

DICK: Will you leave me alone?

HELEN: Come on, Dickie! Don't wreck everything! Come on! Come on! *(She touches his penis)*

BOB: No fair! Damn it!

HELEN *(To Bob)*: You shut up and keep working. *(After a while, to Dick)* You're getting no place, Dick. You're just pathetic. *(She removes her hand)*

DICK: You're a shithead, Helen. *(Helen starts to masturbate with the dildo. Dick watches her for a long while. Then he speaks)* I said you're a shithead.

(He grabs the dildo and throws it across the room. She tries to run to get it, and he grabs her and wrestles her down to the floor and starts hitting her. Grunts and cries. Judy enters. Bob keeps masturbating.)

JUDY: Hi there, Bob.

BOB: Hi, Judy. I'm just doing this.

JUDY: I can see that, Bob. *(She looks at Helen and Dick)* Those disgusting farts. *(To Helen)* I'm taking your little thing, you disgusting vomits.

(She picks up the dildo and licks it. Dick and Helen stop fighting for a moment to look at her, and Helen rushes at her, pulling her to the floor by her hair and hitting her. Dick tries to pull Helen off, and all fight violently. Judy is screaming. She still holds the dildo. Then Bob comes, dripping sperm over the other three, and they stop fighting and separate. Silence for a moment.)

HELEN: Oh, wow——

DICK: God, thanks a lot there, Bob.

(Judy is sitting at some distance on the floor from the others. She begins to masturbate with the dildo, more and more vigorously.)

BOB: Gosh, what a wonderful feeling. I love the way it feels right here, just right at the edge. *(Pointing to the head of his penis)*

HELEN: Hey, my hand is bleeding.

(Judy finally comes, then drops the dildo on the floor.)

BOB: God, it's freezing in here. I hope we don't catch cold!

(Judy exits. Suddenly all feel cold. Bob sneezes loudly, takes a blanket and wraps himself up. Judy enters Room 2 and lies down on the bed. She masturbates with difficulty, manually and with her pillow. Bob leans against a wall of Room 1 and shuts his eyes. Dick washes himself with some water in a corner of the room and finally lies down on the bed. Helen wraps herself in a blanket and gets some food from the big box. She eats it, huddled to the wall. All are shivering. Judy continues to masturbate in Room 2.)

JUDY: It's so unfair. Just so unfair.

(Judy comes, and then sleeps. Long silence. In Room 1, Bob and Dick fall asleep. A long, long silence. Then Tom enters Room 2. He switches on a rather bright light and kisses Judy.)

TOM: Hi, darling.
JUDY: Hi, Tom. *(Waking up)*
TOM: How's my sweet little wife?

JUDY: Am I your wife, darling?

TOM: Of course, my angel. You remember that.

JUDY: I know, Tom.

TOM: I've brought some breakfast. I sure could eat it.

JUDY: So could I, Tom. I'd really love to.

TOM: Here. Fix it yourself. However you like it.

JUDY: Thanks, Tom. That would really be great.

(Judy fixes the breakfast, and they sit at a table and eat it.)

TOM: Smells like sperm in here, Judy. Did you have visitors?

JUDY: Only Bob, darling. He made me do it.

TOM: Bob? He's crazy! I think he's odd—I really do.

JUDY: He is odd, darling. A peculiar person.

TOM: Does he love you, darling?

JUDY: I don't know, Tom. Sometimes I think so. I wish *I* were odder.

TOM: I know, darling—I guess it's difficult.

JUDY: Do you think Bob loves me?

TOM: I'm not sure, sweetheart. He certainly seems to.

JUDY: I'm glad. I like him. I think he's nice.

TOM: But don't you like me, Judy?

JUDY: Yes, but he's nice, too.

TOM: I know, darling. I was only teasing.

JUDY: All right, Tom. I knew you were. *(Pause)* Have some more food.

TOM: Thanks, Judy. *(Silence)* I ran into Baby Naylor last night. He's playing trumpet with Leiku Kanefian.

JUDY: Really, darling?

TOM: Yes—that's what he said.

JUDY: That's great. How nice. What a good position! *(Pause)* Gosh, Tom. I wish *you* had a job. Why *don't* you get one? You know you're qualified.

TOM: I know, Judy. But I just can't concentrate.

JUDY: Does your mother support you, sweetheart?

TOM: You know she does, Judy.

JUDY: I guess I thought perhaps she'd stopped it, Tom.

TOM: But why would she stop it, Judy? That's silly. You know she cares about me.

JUDY: I know that, Tom. I certainly know that, my darling. I know that, baby. I know. I know. I do know that, darling. I know, darling. I know, darling. I know, darling. I know, darling.

TOM: I know you know, Judy. I know that, dear.

(Silence.)

JUDY: Bill—

TOM: I'm Tom, darling.

JUDY: I know you're Tom, sweetheart. I was just talking to you.

TOM: I know, darling.

JUDY: Tom—don't you think we should clear out some of our odds and ends, darling? Our possessions have accumulated so. There are so many things we don't even need.

TOM: Or want. That's true. Really. Let's chuck them all out.

JUDY: But Tom—don't you like our things?

TOM: Well—I don't know, darling. Not really too many of them. They're mostly junk, after all.

JUDY: Well I guess so, darling. I mean, I picked them carefully.

TOM: Well—all the same, I think they're junk.

JUDY: I guess you're right, Tom, and we'd better chuck them out.

TOM: Okay, Judy—if you want to.

JUDY: If I want to?

TOM: Well—it was your idea.

JUDY: Well—I suppose it was, darling, but it was really your idea.

TOM: Well, I suppose it was, darling, but it was really your idea.

JUDY: Well, it was really your idea, darling. But let's throw them all out. *(Silence)* Tom?

TOM: What?

JUDY: You're in a bad mood, sweetheart. What's the matter?

TOM: Nothing's the matter.

JUDY: No, really, darling.

TOM: I'm sick of my job. The goddamned boss gets into my hair.

JUDY: But Tom, I don't—

TOM: Crosses me every chance he gets. Damned son of a bitch.

JUDY: You don't have a job, Tom. I wish you did.

TOM: Well so do I, damn it. So why are you stopping me, then?

JUDY: I'm not stopping you, Tom.

TOM: You liar—don't you say you're not stopping me.

JUDY: Don't say it, Tom?

TOM: I said, don't say it. *(He slaps her)*

JUDY: Okay, Tom. You win. You win.

TOM: You bet I win, baby. That's what winning's all about.

(Long silence. Then he hits her again. They fight violently on the bed. Long silence. In Room 1, Helen shifts her position against the wall, still cold and shivering. Long silence. Tom is almost asleep. Then Judy gets up, touches her face.)

JUDY: Well well. Hey, Tom, you know you've wounded me? You've really harmed me.

TOM: What?

JUDY: I say, you've really harmed me.

TOM: I have?

JUDY: But not too interested?

TOM: I thought I was sleeping.

JUDY: I think you're an asshole, Tom.

TOM: I thought I was sleeping.

JUDY: Are these dreams, Tom? I really feel bruised. These cuts really hurt. You've finally hurt me, Tom.

TOM: "You've finally hurt me, Tom."

JUDY: Do you like me, Tommy? Do you actually like me?

TOM: Your mouth is open, Judy.

JUDY: Do you like me? Do you like me? *(Pause)* "Here we finally are, Judy." "I think I understand you, Judy."

(Silence. She shudders. Silence. Blackout.)

MR. FRIVOLOUS

An appealing room. Mr. Frivolous, a man in his early thirties. Breakfast on a table. Mr. Frivolous is about to pour some coffee for himself.

MR. FRIVOLOUS: Mmm—yum yum yum—now for a good cup of coffee. *(The coffee spills)* Whoops. *(Pause)* I guess it—yes. *(He wipes up the spill. He pours the coffee again and sips it)* I always ask these mornings why, I always ask why the birds always flutter by the curtain just as the sun dips behind a cloud. Darker, darker. They're so loud—they might be in the room. *(Pause)* I ask the little bird why he stays, he says he's going away. He asks why wait, why not fly, now, down to the water, down to that bubbling water, down by the sand. *(Pause)* It's cold and cloudy. What a terrible breeze. *(Pause)* I step on a stair of grass, running with water. I stand on the water, my shoes barely wet, the trees on each side passing, clouds dark with rain, waiting to pour. *(He looks at*

75

the food on the table) I don't feel like this. Let's get this stuff out of the way. Now. *(He moves the food)* I'm tired. Yes. And a little bit sick. I'm sorry. You don't find it appealing. I'm sorry. I'm sorry. I'm sorry. I'm sorry. *(Pause)* I asked you once, who flies with the crow. Where do they both go. Why the sky is gray where the crow flies, why I'm tucked in the corner of his wing, a pilot, watching the earth, like a jewel on a ring. Dogs are mating outside. Come into the garden! You can see—there. Lettuce, dirt. Just a few little flowers. *(Pause)* And I wonder, who are you, my darling, what are you? Yes, I'm awakened by a late-night telephone call, make my way from bed, grabbing a blanket and a cushion, to speak to you. The room is cold. And you too lie in darkness, far from me. I'm stretched out on the floor, and I beg you, Come get me now. Please, come find me. I lie here naked, I lie here waiting. Waiting. Waiting. Now. Now. Now. Now. I want to be pulled, and looted, and ripped by your nails, painted, like a placard, with your lipstick on my back, my legs, my ass, my asshole. And these things, all these, lying around—these sheets, these bits of clothes, of brassieres, of panties—these are an easel, for all that work. *(Pause)* And then I speak to my priest, and I say, Priest, touch me. Lie down here beside me. *(Pause)* God bless the priests who lie by the side of their lovers, whose arms touch the arms of their lovers, whose prickly cheeks touch the face of their lovers. *(Pause)* And then I remember that long afternoon when with wings unfurled, the angels scattered the light across the grass, and we waited while they did, and ran back to us, and then we sent them out again. You were the littlest angel, you ran under my robe and held my legs. And then finally at dusk we gathered up our clothes, long since discarded as we lay in the grass, and headed for home, to wash, have dinner, tuck you in, and lights out.

(Blackout.)

END

AFTERWORD

WAIT—I FORGOT to say in my introduction that the plays in this book touch on the subject of sex. Actually, it seemed better to comment on that after you'd read the book, the topic of sex being so terribly volatile (so they say) that my comments might possibly have distorted the way you looked at the plays.

For whatever reason, and I don't remember how it happened, I am now what people call "sixty-four years old," and I have to admit that I started writing about sex almost as soon as I realized it was possible to do so—say, at the age of fourteen—and I still do it, even though I was in a way the wrong age then, and in a different way I guess I'm the wrong age now. Various people who have liked me or cared about me—people who believed in my promise as a writer—have hinted to me at different times in my life that an excessive preoccupation with the subject of sex has harmed or even ruined my writing. They've implied that it was sad, almost pitiful, that an adolescent obsession—or maybe it was in fact a psychological compulsion—should have been allowed to marginalize what they optimistically had hoped might have been a serious body of work. Meanwhile, people I don't know very well have tended over all those decades to break into a very particular smile, one I recognize now, when they've learned that I've written something that deals with sex—a winking smile which seems to suggest that a trivial, silly, but rather amusing topic has been mentioned. It's a smile not unlike the smile that would appear on the faces of some of our more conservative teachers in the 1950s when the topic of "jazz" was raised—a smile sometimes accompanied back in those days by a mocking, suggestive swaying of the hips.

I suppose it goes without saying that James Joyce, D. H. Lawrence and others were expanding the scope of literature and redrawing humanity's picture of itself when they approached this subject in the earlier part of the twentieth century. But by the time I came along, many of my friends were embarrassed on my behalf precisely because the topic I was writing about seemed so closely associated with an earlier era.

So why *have* I stuck with it? I suppose it has to do with the point I've heard boringly expressed by writers in one way or another all of my life—the thing they always say, while in a way always hoping that no one will believe them, though what they're saying is true—some variation or another of "*I don't do my own writing.*" I personally sometimes express the point, when pressed, by saying that I see my writing as a sort of collaboration between my rational self ("me") and the voice that comes from outside the window, the voice that comes in through the window, whose words I write down in a state of weirded-out puzzlement, thinking, "Jesus Christ, what the fuck is he saying?"

The collaboration is really quite an unequal partnership, I'd have to admit. The voice contributes everything, and

I contribute nothing, frankly, except some modest organiz-
ing abilities and (if I may say so) a certain skill in finding,
among the voice's many utterances, those that are most successful. (I suppose I'm quite a bit like one of those young college graduates in jacket and tie who help some unruly but
for some reason celebrated man to write his autobiography.)
But when I try to define the voice, I say, weakly, "Oh, that's
the unconscious." And eventually, if I brood about it, I'm
forced to conclude that, if the unconscious has thoughts, it
has to have heard these thoughts, or at least their constituent
fragments, from human beings of some description—from
the people I've met, the people I've read about, the people
I've happened to overhear on the street. So it's not just a the-
ory that society is speaking to itself through me. If it were
not so, all I would be able to hear, and all I would be trying
to transcribe, would be the sound of my own heart sending
blood through my veins.

Obviously society has asked writers, as a group, to take
time out from normal labor to do this special listening and
transcribing, and each individual writer has been assigned a
certain part of the spectrum. No writer knows—or *can*
know—whether the section that's been assigned to him con-
tains the valuable code that will ultimately benefit the human
species or whether his section consists merely of the more
common noise or chatter. But obviously the system can only
work if everyone dutifully struggles to do his best with the
material that's been given to him, rather than trying to do
what has already been assigned to somebody else.

The voice outside my own particular window has
repeatedly come back to the subject of sex. And sure, I regret
it in a way, or it sometimes upsets me. But if I were to conclude that the voice is fundamentally not to be trusted,
where would I be then? The enterprise of writing would
have to come to an end for me, because on what basis could

I possibly decide to reject what the voice was saying so insistently? The truth is that, even if I wanted to reject *my* voice and try to listen to somebody else's, I wouldn't be able to hear it. And without an outside voice, what would I write down? Who would I listen to? "Me?" It doesn't work that way. So at a certain point—and with a certain sadness, because of how I knew I would be seen by other people—I decided I was going to trust the voice I was hearing. And of course, like every writer, I hope I'll be one of the ones who will be led to do something truly worthwhile. But in another way, it actually doesn't matter whether it's me or not. That's just a game—who did the best? The actually important question is not whether "I" am one of the better cogs in the machine—the important question is whether the whole mechanism of which I'm a part is or is not one of evolution's cleverer species-survival devices, one that might be very helpful—even at the last minute.

Why is sex interesting to write about? To some, that might seem like a rather dumb question. Obviously when someone interested in geology is alone in a room, he or she tends to think a lot about rocks. And I imagine that when many geologists were children, they put pictures having to do with rocks on their bedroom walls. And I would have to guess that geologists find it fun to sit at a desk and write about rocks. So, yes, I find it enjoyable. But apart from that, I still find myself wondering, "Why is it interesting to write about sex?"

One reason is that sex is shocking. Yes, it's still shocking, after all these years —isn't that incredible? At least it's shocking to me. And I suppose I think it's shocking because, even after all these years, most bourgeois people, including me, still walk around with an image of themselves in their heads that doesn't include—well—*that*. I'm vaguely aware that while going about my daily round of behavior I'm making use of various mammalian processes, such as breathing, digesting, and getting from place to place by hobbling about on those odd legs we have. But the fact is that when I form a picture of myself, I see myself doing the sorts of things that humans do and *only* humans do—things like hailing a taxi, going to a restaurant, voting for a candidate in an election, or placing receipts in various piles and adding them up. But if I'm unexpectedly reminded that my soul and body are capable of being totally swept up in a pursuit and an activity that pigs, flies, wolves, lions and tigers also engage in, my normal picture of myself is violently disrupted.

Writing about sex is really a variant of what Wordsworth did, that is, it's a variant of writing about nature, or as we call it now, "the environment." Sex is "the environment" coming inside, coming into our home or apartment and taking root inside our own minds. It comes out of the mud where the earliest creatures swam; it comes up and appears in our brains in the form of feelings and thoughts. It sometimes appears with such great force that it sweeps other feelings and other thoughts completely out of the way. And on a daily basis it quietly and patiently approaches the self and winds itself around it and through it until no part of the self is unconnected to it.

Sex is really an extraordinary meeting of the meaningful and the meaningless. The big toe, for example, is one part of the human body, human flesh shaped and constructed in a particular way. The penis is another part of the body, located not too far away from the big toe and built out of fundamentally the same materials. The act of sex, the particular shapes of the penis and the vagina, are the way they are because natural selection has made them that way. There may be an adaptive value to each particular choice that evolution made, but from our point of view as human beings living our lives, the evolutionary explanations are unknown, and the various details present themselves to us as completely arbitrary. It can only be seen as funny that men buy magazines containing pictures of breasts, but not magazines with pictures of knees or elbows. It can only be seen as funny that demagogues give speeches denouncing men who insert their penises into other men's anuses—and then go home to insert their own penises into their wives' vaginas! (One might have thought it obvious that either both of these acts are completely outrageous, or neither of them is.) And yet the interplay and permutations of the apparently meaningless, the desire to penetrate anus or vagina, the glimpse of the naked breast, the hope of sexual intercourse or the failure of it, lead to joy, grief, happiness or desperation for the human creature.

Perhaps it is the power of sex that has taught us to love the meaningless and thereby turn it into the meaningful. Apparently, amazingly, the love of what is arbitrary (which one could alternately describe as the love of reality) is something we human beings are capable of feeling (and perhaps even what we call the love of the beautiful is simply a particular way of exercising this remarkable ability). So it might not be absurd to say that if you love the body of another person, if you love another person, if you love a meadow, if you love a horse, if you love a painting or a piece of music or the sky at night, then the power of sex is flowing through you.

It is often noted that writers like to write about conflict, and of course conflict is built into the theme of sex. A story about a person who wants to have a plate of spaghetti might be interesting, but a story about a person who wants to have another person—now, that is potentially even *more* interesting, because the person who is desired may not want to participate. But even leaving aside the conflict involved in the fact that people's desires are often at cross purposes, sex has always been known to be such a powerful force that fragile humanity can't help but be terribly nervous in front of it, so powerful barriers have been devised to control it—taboos of all varieties, first of all, and then all the emotions subsumed under the concepts of jealousy and possessiveness, possessiveness being a sort of anticipatory form of jealousy. (I noticed recently that a sociological survey of married people in the United States found that when asked the question: "What is very important for a successful marriage?" the quality mentioned most frequently—by 93% of the respondents—was "faithfulness," while "happy sexual relationship" came in with only 70%. In other words, to 23% of the respondents, it seemed more important that they and their partner should *not* have sex with others than that they themselves should enjoy sex.) Sex seems capable of creating anarchy, and those who are committed to predictability and order find themselves inevitably either standing in opposition to it, or occasionally trying to pretend to themselves that it doesn't even exist. My local newspaper, *The New York Times*, for example, does not include images of naked people. Many of its readers might enjoy it much much more if it did, but those same people still might not buy it if those images were in it, because if it contained such images it couldn't be *The New York Times*, it couldn't present the portrait of a normal, stable, adequate world—a world not ideal, but still good enough—which it's the function of *The New York Times* to present every day. Nudity somehow seems to imply that anything could happen, but *The New York Times* is committed to telling its readers that many things will *not* happen, because the world is under control, benevolent people are looking out for us, the situation is not as bad as we tend to think, and while problems do exist, they can be solved by wise rulers. The contemplation of nudity or sex could tend to bring up the alarming idea that at any moment human passions might rise up and topple the world we know.

But perhaps it would be a good thing if people saw themselves as a part of nature, connected to the environment in which they live. Sex can be a very humbling, equalizing force. It's often been noted that naked people do not wear medals, and weapons are forbidden inside the pleasure garden. When the sexuality of the terrifying people we call "our leaders" is for some reason revealed, they lose some of their power—sometimes all of it—because we're reminded (and strangely, we need reminding) that they are merely creatures like the ordinary worm or beetle that creeps along at the edge of the pond. Sex really is a nation of its own. Those whose allegiance is given to sex at a certain moment withdraw their loyalty temporarily from other powers. It's a symbol of the possibility that we might all defect for one reason or another from the obedient columns in which we march.

February 2008